Good Jobs, Bad Jobs, No Jobs

Tough Choices for Canadian Labor Law

Roy J. Adams
Gordon Betcherman
Beth Bilson

with comments by
Roger Phillips
and
John O'Grady

The Social
Policy Challenge 10

John Richards
and
William G. Watson,
Series Co-Editors

C.D. Howe Institute

C.D. Howe Institute publications are available from:
Renouf Publishing Company Limited, 1294 Algoma Road,
Ottawa, Ontario K1B 3W8; phone (613) 741-4333; fax (613) 741-5439

and from Renouf's stores at:
71½ Sparks Street, Ottawa (613) 238-8985
211 Yonge Street, Toronto (416) 363-3171

For trade book orders, please contact:
McGraw-Hill Ryerson Limited, 300 Water Street,
Whitby, Ontario L1N 9B6; phone (416) 430-5050

Institute publications are also available in microform from:
Micromedia Limited, 165 Hôtel de Ville, Place du Portage, Phase II,
Hull, Quebec J8X 3X2

This book is printed on recycled, acid-free paper.

Canadian Cataloguing in Publication Data

Adams, Roy J.
    Good jobs, bad jobs, no jobs : tough choices
for Canadian labor law

(The social policy challenge ; 10)
Includes bibliographical references.
ISBN 0-88806-3352-0

1. Labor market – Canada. 2. Manpower policy –
Canada. 3. Labor law and legislation – Canada.
4. Labor market. 5. Manpower policy.
I. Betcherman, Gordon. II. Bilson, Beth, 1946–
III. C.D. Howe Institute. IV. Series

HD5728.A33 1995   331.12′0971   C95-932102-0

Cover design by Leroux Design Inc.
Printed in Canada by Kromar Printing Ltd.,
Winnipeg, Manitoba, September 1995.

Contents

Foreword

This volume is the tenth in the C.D. Howe Institute's "The Social Policy Challenge," one of the most ambitious series of publications in its history. The 15 studies in the series range from workfare to pensions, from unemployment insurance (UI) to workers' compensation, from housing to aboriginal concerns.

The publication of this series is a daunting task not just for its scope, but also for the urgency and importance of the issues it addresses. Canada needs to modernize its basic social programs — programs that were conceived in an era of economic growth and expanding benefits for the recipients of ever-multiplying public services.

Like many other Canadians, I believe the time is right for a wholesale re-examination of this country's social policies. There are several reasons why.

First, Canada's fiscal situation remains perilous: despite rapid economic growth, the combined borrowing of Ottawa and the provinces still amounts to about $60 billion annually. Such high deficits mean that Canada's debt will continue to grow more quickly than its economic output, which in turn means the ratio of debt to gross domestic product (GDP) will keep on rising, as it has without exception since 1977. With still higher debt-to-GDP ratios, interest payments will consume an even greater share of public budgets, and the country's finance ministers will remain at the mercy of swings in interest rates.* We do not necessarily have to reduce the debt ratio — though our children would appreciate it if we did — but we must stop it from growing.

---

* See Thomas E. Kierans and William B.P. Robson et al., *The Courage to Act: Fixing Canada's Budget and Social Policy Deficits*, C.D. Howe Institute Commentary 64 (Toronto: C.D. Howe Institute, October 1994).

Expenditures on social programs are such an important part of public spending that a re-evaluation of how they work simply must be part of the solution.

Second, Canada is at a crossroads. The phrase is, of course, a rhetorician's reflex. Hardly a year goes by without someone's publishing a volume with that title. And to some extent the cliché is always appropriate: modern democracies make policy decisions almost daily, so they are continually at a crossroads. Still, 1995 will likely see changes to federal-provincial transfers — and possibly the taxing powers of the two levels of government as well.

Everything is on the table for discussion. No doubt, a consensus is developing that Canada has hit the ceiling when it comes to taxes. Even Canadians of the middle-of-the-road variety are no longer willing to finance the apparently unending expansion of the welfare state into more and more marginal activities.

Third, there is increasing concern that many of the programs Canadian governments have put in place over the years may not be good for the people they are supposed to help. Within the academic community, it is now respectable to speak of "transfer dependency," a concept for which economist Thomas Courchene was widely criticized when he introduced it into the Canadian debate in the 1970s. Politicians and commentators across the ideological spectrum now agree that policies that were introduced for very good short-term reasons have created harmful long-term incentives. For example, many Canadians have changed their lifestyles to conform to the rules of the UI and welfare systems. As the growth of Ontario's welfare caseload illustrates, transfer dependency may no longer be a problem exclusive to the Atlantic region.

Canadians and their governments thus are likely to be preoccupied with social policy over the next few years. It is with this in mind that the C.D. Howe Institute decided to undertake this in-depth examination of social programs. In choosing the co-editors of the series — John Richards, Associate Professor of Business Administration at Simon Fraser University, and William Watson, Associate Professor of Economics, McGill University

— I sought to bring a balance of views to the Institute's work. John Richards was a member of Allan Blakeney's New Democratic government in Saskatchewan in the early 1970s. William Watson terms himself "a member of that beleaguered cultural minority, the Canadian right." Although both are experts in the field of economics, neither had previously concentrated his formidable energies in the social policy area, and I felt they would bring a fresh view to some of the same old policy conundrums.

Readers will note that each volume will contain differing, at times opposing, views as to whether a particular social program works as intended, needs fixing, or should be left alone. If the conclusion is that a program does need modernizing, the authors will recommend necessary reforms and ways to bring them about.

The C.D. Howe Institute's aim in presenting this series is to raise the level of public debate on issues of national interest by presenting diverse points of view — whether or not it agrees with them — in publications that are well researched and well grounded. The Institute hopes that, in so doing, it will give Canadians much to think about, including the information they require to exercise their responsibilities as citizens.

This volume was copy edited by Deborah Caruso, Lenore d'Anjou, Freya Godard, and Riça Night, and prepared for publication by Barry A. Norris. The analysis and opinions presented in the study are the responsibility of the authors and do not necessarily reflect the views of the Institute's members or Board of Directors.

Thomas E. Kierans
President and
Chief Executive Officer

The Study in Brief

Why a volume on labor law in a series on social policy? On first reflection, debates over the scope of union and management powers may seem far removed from policy debates on pensions, welfare, or unemployment insurance (UI). But on further thought, it becomes obvious that social policy and labor law are intimately linked in any modern welfare state. One means to appreciate the link is to approach the question historically.

A Little History

In mid-nineteenth century Britain, urban living conditions for the working class were comparable to those of many Third World cities today. The wealthy could avoid the squalor but, as one historian has put it, "epidemics were the working class's revenge" (Harvie 1984, 446). In 1832, a cholera epidemic from the Middle East swept through Europe, killing an estimated 31,000 people in Britain alone. Its victims were primarily the poor, but the wealthy did not escape unscathed. Not surprisingly, such an environment encouraged the evolution of many competing "species" of political organization, and social policy slowly improved

One approach, Chartism, was revolutionary. Although it was the progenitor of a multitude of radical political movements, revolutionary politics became of marginal importance in Britain after 1850. Another approach arose from a demand by country's middle and upper classes for the overhaul of local government and an improvement of its administrative ability to supply social services, and for the regulation of the most blatantly offensive excesses of the market economy. Local boards of health appeared at this time, charged with tasks such as the provision of clean water and sanitary waste disposal. New laws and regulations began to constrain the employment contract. Starting in the

1830s, for example, the Factory Inspectorate limited the ability of textile owners to engage child labor.

A third approach can be found in the growth of self-reliant unions, particularly among the "labor aristocracy" of craftsmen. Among other goals, these unions sought to provide basic social programs for their members. Union-imposed levies financed a range of programs — for example, sickness, unemployment, and burial benefits. Later in the nineteenth century, unions became more interested in the potential role of government in social policy. Leaving aside the revolutionary minority, which had always thought in terms of political power, the reformist majority of British union leaders in time came to argue the case that government should universalize social programs. The rationale was a mixture of redistributive arguments (let's finance universal programs via progressive taxation) and efficiency arguments (let's make participation in social insurance programs mandatory because, on the one hand, it would eliminate "free riding" and thereby realize scale economies and, on the other, it would facilitate pooling of good and bad risks and thereby avoid "adverse selection" problems.)

However far removed from Victorian Britain contemporary Canadian society may be, the contributors to this volume are engaged in contemporary variants on arguments that had already emerged 150 years ago. Beth Bilson is skeptical of the ability of either competitive market forces or collective bargaining to eliminate discrimination. Accordingly, she favors an active judiciary able to intervene and redress discrimination in the workplace. She relies on a critique of liberal market economics that would be quite familiar to advocates of the Factory Acts in the British Parliament of the 1830s. John O'Grady, in citing evidence on the positive effect of collective bargaining in lowering the male-female wage gap, makes arguments analogous to those of Victorian trade union leaders. Never more forcefully than at times when incidents of labor conflict prompted public calls for anti-union laws, these leaders insisted that unions were a valuable institution through which to advance equity and social policy.

Tough Choices

Historically, the conclusion is straightforward: unions in industrial societies — very much including Canada — have been centrally involved in the introduction and expansion of social programs. But today, the role of unions in generating good social policy is not so simple.

The best social policy is, as the saying goes, a good job. In that sense, all government policies bearing on the level of employment and the distribution of market earnings are integral to social policy. Unfortunately, one of the disturbing trends of the past two decades in many major industrialized countries, including Canada, is that the supply of "good jobs" for workers with low formal education has declined relative to demand. The best evidence for this is the decline in real annual earnings among men in the bottom fifth of wage earners — some 16 percent among Canadian men between 1973 and 1989. Roughly half of this decline occurred because of a reduction in the number of hours worked, but even among men who worked full time, full year, real annual earnings of the bottom fifth declined by 7 percent over that period (Morissette et al. 1995, 28).[1]

To quote a recent report by the Organisation for Economic Co-operation and Development (OECD 1994a, 2):

> One clear dimension to structural change has been, and continues to be, a systematic shift away from the employment

---

[1] Among women, the trend is less ominous. Morissette et al. (1995) report a 36 percent increase in real earnings among women in the bottom fifth of wage earners over the 1973–89 period, an increase due primarily to an increase in the number of hours worked by part-time female workers. Among those women who worked full time, full year, incomes fell as they did for men, but proportionately less — 3 percent for women as opposed to 7 percent for men. Full-time, full-year workers are defined as those who worked at least 48 weeks in the year and who worked mainly full time during those weeks.

of low- or narrowly skilled labour, both in manufacturing and in services. This reflects both demand and supply-side factors but the most important cause has apparently been technical progress, which is increasingly being reflected in a move towards a more knowledge-intensive economy. A sharp widening of wage differentials in the United States has preserved employment of some of the unskilled, but at the expense of an increase in in-work poverty; in Europe wage inflexibility has prevented the emergence of in-work poverty, but at the expense of high rates of unemployment of the low-skilled.

The OECD here poses a painful policy choice between the "US" and the "European" options. The "US" option has maintained reasonably full employment and rapid employment growth by increasing wage polarization and eliminating unions from most of the private sector. As recently as 1965, union density (the fraction of nonagricultural employees who belong to a union) was approximately 30 percent in both Canada and the United States.[2] Since then, union density in the United States has been halved. The "European" option has prevented wage dispersion and maintained the status quo with respect to unions, but at the cost of slow employment growth and unacceptably high unemployment, particularly among the young, the low skilled, and immigrants.

So far, Canada has fallen somewhere between these two options. As in the United States, wage dispersion in Canada has increased and employment growth has been rapid relative to Europe. As in Europe, union density levels in Canada have remained at levels that prevailed during the 1960s, and social programs designed to transfer income to those at the bottom have

---

2 Union density in Canada in 1965 was slightly lower than in the United States. Since 1965, union density in the two countries has diverged. In the United States, density has steadily declined, falling to 15.8 percent by 1993, a figure comparable to that of the mid-1930s, before introduction of the *Wagner Act* (which is discussed later in the introduction). In Canada, union density rose until the early 1980s, peaking in 1984 at 39 percent. Since then, it has declined slightly; in 1994, it was 37.5 percent (Canada 1995; Griffiths 1994; Richards 1993).

been expanded. The share of income accruing to the bottom fifth of Canadians has actually increased slightly over the past two decades. Generous UI and social assistance programs have offset the distribution effects that would otherwise have arisen from trends in market earnings.[3] But these programs are very expensive, and contain a variety of perverse incentives against work; consequently, the status quo is not an option. Senior Canadian governments doubtless will introduce major changes over the rest of this decade to both UI and social assistance.

In its *Jobs Study* report, the OECD (1994b) describes a more complex set of labor market alternatives (see the box on the following two pages). Whether one thinks in terms of the simple choice posed above or in terms of choice among a more complex set of options, tough tradeoffs cannot be avoided. With the exception of Beth Bilson, who tackles a somewhat different problem, the writers in this volume are, in effect, debating the nature and magnitude of these tradeoffs. They are attempting to answer the question: Given the tradeoffs involved, what is the optimum set of labor market policies that will maximize the number of "good jobs"?

The Status Quo

There is no point in pretending that the contributors converge on a set of optimal policies. Were they to have done so, it would have been surprising because, quite intentionally, we chose the three major contributors as articulate exponents of divergent strategies. (This is not to slight the commentators; they, too, have well-developed positions to defend.) What the authors have in common is not their solutions but a certain shared dissatisfaction with the dominant current way of doing things and the labor law

---

3 This summary conclusion on trends in income distribution is drawn from Beach and Slotsve, a forthcoming volume in "The Social Policy Challenge" series that surveys trends in income distribution in Canada over the past two decades.

Tough Choices: Five Labor Market Options

The following five broad options are defined in the comprehensive OECD survey *Jobs Study* (OECD 1994b, 25), from which this extract has been taken:

The European Community

Weak employment growth, most of it until the mid-1980s in the public sector, has been accompanied by strong productivity growth, achieved mostly through labour-shedding in traditional sectors rather than through shifts of production to high-technology and skill-intensive activities. Unemployment has ratcheted up over successive cycles, resulting in rising long-term unemployment. Inflows into unemployment have been relatively low but outflows even lower — suggesting poorly functioning labour markets.

The United States

Buoyant growth of both high-skilled and low-skilled jobs in the private sector, especially in services, has been accompanied by weak average productivity growth. Wage differentials have widened, and real wages for the low-paid have fallen absolutely, resulting in growing in-work poverty. Fluctuations in unemployment have been mainly cyclical, with high inflows and outflows, a low incidence of long-term unemployment, and only a moderate trend rise in total unemployment.

---

that underlies it. They insist that we take alternatives seriously and realize that other countries do things differently.

The dominant way of doing things in Canada is described by Gordon Betcherman as "traditional" management, by Roy Adams as "adversarial" industrial relations, and by John O'Grady as "job control unionism." In summary, what the contributors mean by these terms is some combination of the following institutional arrangements:

• *Traditional North American unions.* If present in a firm, unions undertake only those collective bargaining activities sanctioned by the tradition of the 1935 *Wagner Act*, the Magna Carta of union rights on this continent. The act was

Canada/Oceania

As in the United States, employment growth in the private sector has been strong, productivity growth slow, wage differentials have widened, and real wages for low-paid workers have fallen. But there have also been important differences: systems of social protection are more extensive than in the United States; and unions have had more influence in collective bargaining. Most importantly, there has been a strong upward trend in unemployment over the past two decades.

Japan

Japan has managed to maintain low unemployment, as measured. A well-developed internal labour market has enabled firms, in particular large firms, to adjust to structural change by shifting production to higher value-added products, and by up-skilling and redeploying their work forces accordingly. But continuing weak demand is producing clear signs of rising underemployment, either in the form of labour hoarding or of withdrawal, especially of women, from the labour force.

The European Free Trade Association

Strong employment growth has taken place in the public sector, with little or none in the private sector; highly productive industries compete effectively on world markets; and there has tended to be relatively little wage dispersion. Unemployment has for much of the period been relatively low, due to: the role of the public sector as an employer of last resort; bargaining systems that were sensitive to the need to preserve low unemployment; and significant investment in active labour market policies. But when the public sector stopped expanding, unemployment increased rapidly.

an important piece of New Deal legislation in the United States that provided a secure legislative basis to collective bargaining. In the 1940s, Ottawa and the provinces each adopted variants of this act. The *Wagner Act* proclaimed the right of workers "to bargain collectively through representatives of their own choosing." It codified mechanisms whereby a union could obtain the legal monopoly (that is, become certified) to represent a particular group of workers in collective bargaining and formal grievance proceedings. It introduced the concept of unfair labor practices that limit employers' efforts to prevent or evade collective bargaining. And instead of the courts' operating on the basis of the common law, it introduced the concept of a powerful tribunal (labor relations boards) to arbitrate industrial disputes.

- *The management right clause.* Subject to the constraint of the collective bargaining agreement, management preserves an undiluted right to manage the workplace. In practice, most union leaders want no blurring of the line between manager and worker, viewing workers' involvement in management decisions as "collaboration" that threatens their commitment to collective bargaining.

- *Seniority, precise job demarcation and straight wage formulas.* Most large workplaces are characterized by the importance of seniority in determining promotion, wages, and layoffs. While workers may have no formal job security, employers face the threat of serious work stoppages if they attempt to dismiss workers on any basis other than inverse seniority. Furthermore, precisely demarcated job descriptions limit the ability of management to reduce employment by having workers perform multiple tasks. Wages typically are specified per unit of time (dollars per hour or per month), and do not incorporate incentive components based on productivity or net earnings of the firm.

- *Decentralized wage bargaining.* Most wage negotiations take place at the level of the firm. While industry-wide pattern bargaining has emerged (for example, with the Big Three auto manufacturers), employers and unions have resisted centralized corporatist exercises in negotiating wages for an entire state, province, or country. Such practices are viewed with suspicion as wage control. In practice, wage negotiations turn heavily on union attempts to preserve wage relativities by using a wage increase in one bargaining unit as a precedent in others. For complex reasons, strike-lockout rates per unionized worker in the English-speaking countries with this style of wage bargaining have been much higher than in many other OECD countries, such as Germany, the Scandinavian countries, and Japan.

Having introduced the problems, I turn now to a summary of the contributors' arguments and the commentators' responses.

Roy Adams: Promote "Social Partnerships"

For Roy Adams, the status quo has led to excessively adversarial labor-management relations, which, in turn, has led to unnecessarily high unemployment, lost production through high strike-lockout rates, and a denial of any say in the workplace for the nonunionized. Adams divides a sample of 14 OECD countries into two groups, "adversarial" and "social partnership," based on the extent to which industrial relations in each incorporate elements of labor-management cooperation. His seven "adversarial" countries are Canada, the United States, Britain, Australia, France, Italy, and New Zealand; the seven "partnership" countries are Sweden, Germany, Japan, Austria, the Netherlands, and Norway. Averaging over the 1970–92 period, he finds that the "social partnership" countries unambiguously outperform the others. They experience higher average annual per capita real growth in gross domestic product (GDP) (2.7 percent compared with 2.3 percent), lower average annual inflation (5.8 percent compared with 7.3 percent), lower average unemployment rates (3.7 percent compared with 5.2 percent), and dramatically less industrial conflict (45 workdays lost annually per 1,000 workers compared with 210 workdays lost).

Adams' fundamental policy recommendation is that "it would be wise for Canadian policymakers to find ways of moving Canadian industrial relations away from confrontation and toward

consensus" (p. 62). While any such change may well run counter
to the short-run interests of both labor and management, Adams
believes such change is possible. It may be easier, he suggests, at
times when high unemployment, economic recession, or labor
conflict places the legitimacy of the status quo in doubt. In many
countries, business, government, and labor leaders have succeeded, at precisely such moments of severe social tension, in
striking beneficial new "social contracts." Adams favors institutional reforms embedded in law, as opposed to informal conventions. He argues that a prerequisite for consensus is that all
workers in major establishments have collective representation.
This may take the form of union representation, but, in addition
or as a substitute, workers should have access to works councils
with significant powers. Legislating such councils into existence
is a necessary prerequisite for any evolution toward greater
consensus.

To what extent can one attribute the failures of the Canadian
economy to "adversarial" industrial relations? To what extent
could a new more consensual approach improve matters? The
commentators are skeptical.

Both Roger Phillips and John O'Grady refer to Sweden. For
those sympathetic to Adams' case, Sweden has for many years
been a shining example. During the 1990s, however, Sweden has
experienced severe economic and social crisis. Employment has
declined and unemployment has dramatically increased. Major
financial bankruptcies have taken place. The Swedish government, unable to maintain stable exchange rates with other European currencies, was obliged to devalue the krona; generous
social benefits have forced it to incur large deficits; and Sweden's
debt-to-GDP ratio is projected to surpass Canada's in 1995.
Phillips concludes that high-level consensual institutions characteristic of Sweden have hampered that country's ability to adapt.
The Swedish economy performed well for many years, but, faced
with the major shock of the recent recession, it fared worse than the
economies of many other countries: wages could not adjust quickly,

governments could not remove perverse incentives in social programs quickly, and firms could not maintain employment.

As a brief editorial aside, it is important not to throw out the baby with the bathwater. Sweden may not be as shining an example as in previous decades, but aspects of Swedish policy remain attractive. In particular, Swedish "active labor market" policies deserve closer attention as Canadians grapple with the reform of unemployment insurance.

Sweden aside, Phillips and O'Grady are generally skeptical of Adams' thesis. Phillips emphasizes that the superior performance of the "social partnership"countries was primarily a phenomenon of the 1970s. Taking Germany and the United States as the prototype for each class of industrial relations system, he points to convergence during the 1980s. One point of agreement between Phillips and Adams is on the subject of strike-lockout behavior. While Phillips stresses the difficulty in making accurate international comparisons of industrial conflict, he nonetheless agrees with Adams that Canadians should be less complacent about an industrial relations system that generates a remarkably high level of strike-lockout activity by international standards.

Gordon Betcherman: Promote Nontraditional Management Systems

Gordon Betcherman's fundamental critique of the status quo is captured in his concern over the growth of "bad jobs," or what he more formally describes as involuntary nonstandard employment. This

> includes those workforms that depart from the traditional notion of a full-time, relatively permanent attachment to an employer...part-time, short-term (employed for less than six months), and temporary-help work, as well as independent contractors (the self-employed without any employees). (pp. 75–76.)

Why more bad jobs? The reasons are complex. Under "traditional" management, the creation of standard jobs implies that firms incur a more-or-less fixed cost. Expanding nonstandard employment increases management's ability to adjust labor costs to market demand. Furthermore, if a firm is unionized and is paying a wage premium over comparable skill nonunion wages, subcontracting to nonunion firms using nonstandard job design reduces the need for relatively costly union labor. So far this is just a description of divergent interests that unions and management seek to resolve via collective bargaining. There is no reason to expect nonstandard employment to be increasing over time.

The missing variable, Betcherman implies, is government policies "that do not support a strong commitment between employer and employee" (p. 89). One such policy is an unemployment insurance system with generous repeat-use provisions that effectively subsidize firms that resort to nonstandard employment patterns. Second, existing labor laws encourage "traditional" management (here including "job control unionism"), a system which does "not create incentives for firms to adjust internally to changes in labor demand due to a business downturn or technological change" (ibid.). In summary, employers externalize workforce adjustments via layoffs (of low seniority workers) as opposed to internal adjustments that might entail lower wages and reallocation of workers in currently redundant jobs.

The commentators allow, as Phillips expresses it, that "Betcherman is onto something. Nontraditional ILMs [internal labor markets] are arising among growing firms in an increasingly competitive world" (p. 160). He cites as an example the growth of nontraditionally managed steel mills in North America. O'Grady allows that "job control unionism" externalizes the cost of adjustment, which, in turn, has led to the rise of long-term unemployment and higher government costs for social services. Conversely, nontraditional ILMs that emphasize employee participation in management and use flexible compensation systems based on firm performance may be able to increase the proportion of "good jobs" and lower government expenditures related to high rates of unemployment.

As they do with Adams, however, the commentators have serious reservations with Betcherman's thesis. O'Grady suspects that, whatever the compensation system, globalization trends in the economy are pushing firms toward the

> bifurcation of workers into "core" and "periphery" employees. By increasing their reliance on outsourcing and subcontracting, companies that appear to be internalizing adjustment costs may be divesting themselves of those costs through other means....Costs that can be avoided will be avoided. (p. 181.)

High-wage, high-union-density countries in central and northern Europe — despite the prevalence of managerial structures that appear nontraditional by North American criteria — have resorted to subcontracting, frequently to foreign-based firms with lower labor costs. The core employment of "good jobs" has grown much more slowly than the European labor force, resulting in higher rates of long-term unemployment there than in North America.

Phillips raises many subtle arguments that I shall not attempt to summarize, but one in particular deserves mention. Phillips argues that, whatever the faults of North American unions, they are typically better at representing the immediate interests of their members with respect to wages and working conditions than are their European counterparts. When union leaders engage in centralized wage bargaining or strategic corporate management, there may be benefits, but there are also costs. Phillips suspects that North American unions have achieved far more worker autonomy and control over practical matters such as work scheduling than is the case in Europe. As evidence, he refers to the prevalence of nonrecorded "personal" strikes by German union members, who are more dissatisfied with their work conditions than low German strike rates would suggest.

Beth Bilson: The Case
for Judicial Activism

Beth Bilson is interested in a different problem from that underlying the essays of Adams and Betcherman. As briefly mentioned
earlier, she defends the judicial activism that has assumed such
prominence in recent years, particularly since the adoption in
1982 of the Charter of Rights and Freedoms.

To begin, she distinguishes sharply between the traditional
liberal idea of *equality of opportunity* within the market and
equity, an idea related to procedural justice:

> I use "equality" primarily to refer to the liberal notion that
> each citizen has an equivalent stake in society and that each
> person can, therefore, lay claim to a fixed set of rights and
> entitlements. I use "equity," on the other hand, to refer to a
> more dynamic idea: the active consideration of processes or
> structures and the balancing of interests that are required to
> achieve a fairer position for the members of Canadian society
> or of institutions within it. (p. 105, fn 1.)

An important example of this distinction, Bilson suggests, is
found in the historical evolution of ideas about pay equity. In the
nineteenth century, conventional wisdom accepted that it was
just to pay women less than men for identical jobs on grounds
that men had the primary responsibility for the financial support
of their families, whereas women's primary responsibility lay in
the home, raising children. By the middle of the twentieth century, North American jurisdictions had legislated "equal pay for
equal work," and had forbidden employers or unions to use
practices whereby women received less than men for performing
similar work.

But such legislation did not eliminate the raw gap between
average wages for men and women. In Canada, for example, the
earnings of the average woman are still less than two-thirds those
of the average man. Many analysts explain the presence of this
gap in terms of legitimate market factors: men disproportionately

undertake those jobs whose high wages are a reward to risk or unpleasant working conditions; for a given age, the average man has more job experience than the average women because men tend not to leave the workforce for child rearing; while the gap is narrowing, men still have, on average, more training than women. Modern feminists, including Bilson, are quick to challenge the adequacy — and complacency — of such explanations:

> The definitions of specific job classifications, however, are to some extent contaminated by social constructions of gender or race....[A] striking example: the value allotted to the skill involved in using a screwdriver but not a syringe and the calculation of extra recompense for "men's dirt" such as axle grease, but not for the vomit and urine encountered by [primarily female] health care workers....
>
> In the increasingly bureaucratic organization of the modern workplace, I believe that the exercise of preferences in the selection and advancement of employees has become insulated from the direct discipline of market forces to a significant extent. Though, in general terms, the market may "punish" an enterprise for making choices that do not rest on "real" considerations related to efficiency and productivity, the bureaucratic structure of many organizations surely creates a great deal of room for making decisions in which assumptions related to race, gender, or physical ability have an influence. (pp. 117–118.)

Thus, for Bilson, it is entirely appropriate that society's concept of equality evolve beyond "equal pay for equal work" to embrace "equal pay for work of equal value," and employment equity (that is, requirements that the distribution of a firm's workforce be similar in terms of race and gender to that of the population) and that courts or administrative tribunals enjoy legislated power to intervene in these matters. There must be, Bilson allows in conclusion, some limit on the resort to law — society must leave room for the processes of political and market accommodation to operate. But overall, the active intervention of human rights tribunals and the courts over the past generation has been beneficial, she concludes.

The commentators are less sure that the right balance has been struck between markets (including here the outcome of collective bargaining) and "rights-based litigation." O'Grady cites evidence on the positive role of multi-employer collective bargaining in narrowing the male-female wage gap. He is dubious that the elaborate pay and employment equity programs in provinces such as Ontario will achieve better results than would collective bargaining, if left to its own devices. In discussing employment equity, Phillips poses three fundamental objections. First, "[a]ny administrative system of job evaluation is highly subjective" (p. 161). Second, "[j]ob evaluation systems require an expensive bureaucracy" (ibid.). Finally, pay equity becomes, in practice, a euphemism for wage increases because it is never broached in terms of lowering wages for "overpaid" males but solely in terms of raising them for "underpaid" females.

The contributors to this volume do not converge on a set of optimal industrial relations policies. What they do have in common is a certain shared dissatisfaction with the dominant current way of doing things. At times, they may appear simply to be arguing at cross purposes, but collectively they have made a useful contribution to an underexplored dimension of social policy.

John Richards

References

Beach, C., and G. Slotsve. Forthcoming. *Are We Becoming Two Societies? Income Polarization and the Middle Class in Canada*, The Social Policy Challenge 11. Toronto: C.D. Howe Institute.

Canada. 1995. *Directory of Labour Organizations in Canada 1994–1995*. Ottawa: Department of Human Resources Development, Bureau of Labour Information.

Gifford, C. 1994. *Directory of US Labor Organizations, 1994–95 Edition*. Washington, DC: Bureau of National Affairs.

Harvie, C. 1984. "Revolution and the Rule of Law (1789–1851)." In K.O. Morgan, ed., *The Oxford Illustrated History of Britain*. Oxford: Oxford University Press.

Morissette, R., et al. 1995. "Earnings Polarization in Canada, 1969–1991." In K. Banting and C. Beach, eds., *Labour Market Polarization and Social Policy Reform*. Kingston, Ont.: Queen's University, School of Policy Studies.

OECD. 1994a. "The OECD Jobs Study." Summary. *OECD Economic Outlook* 55. June.

———. 1994b. The OECD Jobs Study: Facts, Analysis, Strategies. Paris: Organisation for Economic Co-operation and Development.

Richards, J. 1993. "Unions in Canada and the United States: A Tangled Tale." In D. Thomas, ed., *Canada and the United States: Differences that Count*. Peterborough, Ontario: Broadview Press.

From Adversarialism to Social Partnership:
Lessons from the Experience of Germany, Japan, Sweden, and the United States

Roy J. Adams

In the decades since World War II and especially since the 1970s, Canada has had one of the highest rates of industrial conflict among all of the advanced industrialized countries (Lacroix 1986). The rate is indicative of the generally adversarial nature of Canadian labor relations. Various commissions, government agencies, and independent experts have issued a continual stream of calls for labor, management, and the state to move beyond confrontation to social partnership (see, for example, Dodge 1978; Ontario 1984; Riddell 1986; Porter 1991; Canadian Labour Market and Productivity Centre 1993). But progress in that direction has been slow.

The failure to achieve partnership has been costly. A long line of research supports the proposition that nations capable of

Research reported in this paper was initially undertaken for the Canadian Labour Market and Productivity Centre. That work resulted in "Labour, Management, Government Relations and Socioeconomic Performance," a working paper that was distributed in 1992. This essay is a revised version of that paper. Some of the material reported in the original paper was also incorporated into Adams 1995. I am indebted to John Windmuller, Bob Flanagan, Bernie Adell, Derwyn Sangster, John Richards, Daniel Schwanen, Bill Watson, and George Nikitsas for useful comments on the earlier versions of this paper. The final product is, of course, entirely my responsibility.

achieving consensus generally outperform those that remain mired in discordance and adversarialism (see, for example, Barber and McCallum 1982; Treu 1992; Wilensky 1992 and forthcoming). Data in Table 1 are relevant to that proposition. Thirteen advanced, industrialized countries are classified into two categories: *social partnership* or *adversarial*. As a group, those nations with consensual labor relations institutions have performed much better during the past two decades in combining economic growth, price stability, and low unemployment than have the adversarial nations. Indeed, the best performer among the adversarial countries, the United States, performs no better than the worst performer among the social partnership countries, the Netherlands. Table 2 indicates that the consensual nations' performance advantage has continued during the past decade. Six of the seven adversarial nations performed worse than the poorest-performing social partnership country. The two tables also indicate that the consensus countries have, as a group, achieved a very low level of industrial conflict compared with the level in confrontational countries. That observation is very important, because there is a strong relationship between socioeconomic performance and industrial conflict (Barber and McCallum 1982; Wilensky 1992 and forthcoming). Between 1970 and 1992, variation in days lost to industrial conflict "explains" over 60 percent of the variation in the index of socioeconomic performance.[1]

Labor-management-government cooperation is superior to discord for many good reasons. At the national level, accord permits wage bargaining in cooperative countries to be coordinated with fiscal and monetary policy decisions taken by government, whereas adversarial nations enjoy little or no such coordination. Cooperation and bargaining coordination in turn promote a better combination of price stability and high employment. In the adversarial nations, on the other hand, government is commonly

---

[1] When the index of socioeconomic performance reported in Table 1 is regressed on days lost due to industrial conflict — also reported in Table 1 — the R^2 is 0.61.

Table 1: *Socioeconomic Performance in Social Partnership and Adversarial Countries, 1970–92*

	Growth[a] (A)	Inflation[b] (B)	Unemployment[c] (C)	Socioeconomic Performance Index[d]	Days Lost to Industrial Conflict[e]
	(percent)	*(percent)*	*(percent)*		
Social Partnership Countries					
Sweden	1.6	8.1	2.3	11.1	104.1
Germany	2.6	3.8	4.6	14.1	32.4
Japan	3.8	5.4	2.1	16.2	39.4
Austria	3.0	4.8	2.6	15.6	5.2
Netherlands	1.9	4.7	8.1	9.1	22.8
Norway	3.1	7.7	2.7	12.7	65.6
Mean	*2.7*	*5.8*	*3.7*	*13.2*	*44.9*
Adversarial Countries					
United States	1.8	6.0	6.6	9.1	205.0
Canada	2.5	6.6	8.2	7.8	571.0
United Kingdom	1.8	9.6	6.3	6.0	262.5
Australia	2.0	8.4	5.9	7.6	366.9
France	2.4	7.4	6.8	8.1	97.8
Italy	2.9	11.0	8.4	3.4	677.5
New Zealand	1.0	10.6	3.4	7.0	280.3
Mean	*2.1*	*8.5*	*6.5*	*7.0*	*351.6*
Grand mean	*2.3*	*7.3*	*5.2*	*9.9*	*210.0*

Sources: Organisation for Economic Co-operation and Development, *OECD Economic Outlook, Historical Statistics*; idem, *OECD Labour Force Statistics*; International Labour Organisation, *Yearbook of Labour Statistics*.

[a] Real GDP per capita, average year-to-year percentage changes.
[b] Consumer Price Indices, average annual percentage changes.
[c] Average rate of unemployment as a percentage of total labor force.
[d] The sum of B subtracted from 10, plus C subtracted from 10, plus A.
[e] Working days lost per thousand workers.

Table 2: Socioeconomic Performance in Social Partnership and Adversarial Countries, 1983–92

	Growth[a] (A)	Inflation[b] (B)	Unemployment[c] (C)	Socioeconomic Performance Index[d]	Days Lost to Industrial Conflict[e]
	(percent)	(percent)	(percent)		
Social Partnership Countries					
Sweden	1.4	6.7	2.6	12.1	83.3
Germany	3.0	2.2	6.8	13.9	28.9
Japan	3.8	1.8	2.5	19.6	4.2
Austria	2.6	3.0	3.5	16.0	3.7
Netherlands	2.1	2.0	9.3	10.8	12.9
Norway	2.8	5.7	3.8	13.3	89.8
Mean	2.6	3.6	4.8	14.3	37.1
Adversarial Countries					
United States	2.7	3.8	6.7	12.2	75.7
Canada	2.5	4.4	9.6	8.5	344.6
United Kingdom	2.0	5.5	8.4	8.1	113.5
Australia	2.3	6.5	8.1	7.7	190.4
France	1.9	4.4	9.7	7.8	39.7
Italy	2.8	7.5	10.7	4.6	278.9
New Zealand	1.2	8.0	6.5	6.8	304.6
Mean	2.2	5.7	8.5	7.9	192.5
Grand mean	2.4	4.7	6.8	10.9	120.8

Sources: Organisation for Economic Co-operation and Development, *OECD Economic Outlook*, *Historical Statistics*; idem, *OECD Labour Force Statistics*; International Labour Organisation, *Yearbook of Labour Statistics*.

[a] Real GDP per capita, average year-to-year percentage changes.
[b] Consumer Price Indices, average annual percentage changes.
[c] Average rate of unemployment as a percentage of total labor force.
[d] The sum of B subtracted from 10, plus C subtracted from 10, plus A.
[e] Working days lost per thousand workers.

required to pursue or allow high unemployment as a check on wage-price inflation because of the absence of mechanisms for achieving accord (Soskice 1994).[2]

Where labor organizations are fully recognized at the industry level as representing all relevant workers, a technical prerequisite for cooperation at that level is met. Confrontational nations experience less employer willingness to participate in such structures: labor protest, not cooperation, typically results.

During the past decade, a large body of research has strongly affirmed the proposition that labor-management cooperation at the enterprise and workplace level is critical to competitiveness in the 1990s and will remain so into the twenty-first century (Levine and Tyson 1990; Womack, Jones, and Roos 1990; United States 1993). It is widely acknowledged that Japanese labor practices, strongly embedded in labor-management consensus, have been a critical element in the success of Japanese business during the past two decades. As a result, companies throughout the West are attempting to emulate the essential characteristics of that strategy.

This essay reviews the experience of two nations (Germany and Japan) that have stabilized a social partnership after over-

---

2 Research reported in the middle 1980s suggested that both "corporatist" countries in which there was centralized bargaining and countries with decentralized bargaining did better than those with a middling assortment of institutions. Since there is a good deal of overlap between countries that are classified as "corporatist" and those classified as nonadversarial, the proposition was that performance was high both in cooperative countries with centralized bargaining and in adversarial countries (such as the United States) with decentralized bargaining. More recent research, however, distinguishes countries with decentralized bargaining that is coordinated (such as Japan and Switzerland) from those with uncoordinated decentralized bargaining (such as the United States and Canada). Wage setting in the coordinated decentralized countries is much more similar to centralized wage setting than it is to the processes in uncoordinated decentralized countries. Thus, it is argued, the coordinated decentralized countries should more properly be classified with the centralized countries. When that is done, the U-shaped curve disappears and the superiority of coordinated efforts stands out sharply. It also turns out that labor-management relations in coordinated decentralized systems are more consensual than they are in uncoordinated decentralized systems. (See especially Soskice 1994.)

coming very conflictive relations earlier in the century, one nation (Sweden) that enjoyed the fruits of social consensus for many decades before falling back into conflict in the 1980s and 1990s, and one country (the United States) that achieved only a brief, weak accord. The object is to extract lessons relevant for Canada. At a 1984 talk sponsored by the Ontario Ministry of Labour, John McCallum reviewed the evidence on the superiority of cooperation over confrontation and concluded that it would be much better if Canadian practice was more consensual. He then asked, "But how do we do that? I don't really know. How did the other countries do that?" (Ontario 1984, 30). This essay addresses those questions.

Germany

Socioeconomic Performance

Germany has been much studied by international economists and industrial relations experts because of its enormous success, especially in the post–World War II era (see Adams and Rummel 1977; Streeck 1984a, 1984b; Helm 1986; Berghahn and Karsten 1987; Fuerstenberg 1987; Thelen 1987, 1991; Turner 1991).

Despite losing the war and having its economy largely destroyed and its territorial integrity compromised, West Germany had, by the 1980s, established itself as Europe's economic engine. Germany attained that high level of economic performance and competitiveness in the context of a substantial societal consensus, very low levels of industrial conflict, and one of the best records in the West for controlling inflation. It also built an extensive social welfare system that ensured cradle-to-grave security. From the 1950s until the early 1980s, there was full employment. But the deep recession/depression of the early 1980s resulted in a major rise in unemployment that persisted throughout the decade. Moreover, the collapse of communism and the reintegration of East Germany generated an economic burden of much greater dimensions than was originally envisioned.

Business-Labor-Government Relations

A number of key elements in the development of the German system have come to define the relationships between business, labor, and governments at the national, sectoral, and enterprise/workplace levels.

The Legien-Stinnes Accord

As in most nations that are now advanced liberal democracies, employers in Germany initially opposed the formation of independent trade unions. Most insisted on retaining complete control over all aspects of production, including employment relations, in order to compete effectively. Because of pressure from an insurgent labor movement that began in the 1870s and because of the difficulties experienced in Britain during the Industrial Revolution, governments encouraged voluntary cooperation between employers and elected representatives. From the 1890s onward, this led to experiments with employee representation plans. Legislation requiring consultation was passed in the 1890s, after which many companies experimented with employer-initiated representation plans.

When the mainstream of the labor movement adopted the objective of replacing capitalism with socialism, it was opposed vigorously by both government and business. From 1878 through 1890, all socialist organizations were illegal.

When Germany entered World War I, both business and labor initially supported the government. But as the war wore on, labor unrest grew. In 1918, the Kaiser abdicated and fled the country. He was replaced by a social democratic government. Amid the chaos and under pressure from this new government, the central organizations of labor and business signed the Legien-Stinnes Accord in 1918 (Grebing 1969; Berghahn and Karsten 1987; Slomp 1990). The employers agreed to recognize the unions as the legitimate representatives of workers generally and also agreed to stop trying to dissuade individual employees from becoming union members. They also agreed to negotiate wages and other conditions of employment with the unions on an industry basis.

Multi-employer bargaining was sought by both labor and management. The unions wanted that format because it allowed them to serve the widest range of workers. The employers preferred it because such negotiations would concentrate on basic terms and conditions of employment and on general increases, allowing them to maintain considerable discretion at the enterprise and plant levels.

Codetermination

From early in their history, a key object of German unions involved achieving industrial democracy as a natural and essential counterpart of political democracy. But German employers adamantly opposed dealing with unions on a daily basis in the shop. They argued that they needed discretion to make quick decisions free from constraint in order to operate the production process efficiently and effectively. They also argued that the unions' political agenda, if manifested in the shop, would disrupt the production process.

These opposed positions resulted in a compromise. Employers recognized employees' right to representation at the enterprise level; unions recognized that the right to representation should be universal — that is, it should be available to all employees, not just to union members. Legislation putting these principles into effect was passed. It required the establishment of works councils elected by all employees in a company, even if they were not union members or supporters. These councils were to have legally specified rights and duties. Unions could nominate candidates in works council elections, but one did not have to be a union member to stand for election. The legislation also required that workers have a minority representation on corporate supervisory boards.

Neither the unions nor the employers were entirely happy with this compromise. It contained positive and negative aspects from both perspectives. Labor leaders, fearing that the councils might become competitors for employees' allegiance, insisted that unions retain the exclusive right to negotiate wages, hours, and other basic conditions of work. In fact, most of those elected to works councils were active trade unionists. Many nonunionists who were elected joined a union subsequently because of the training and consultative services available from the unions.

For management, being compelled to deal with employee representatives on a day-to-day basis was hard to accept. But dealing with local leaders elected by their peers was considered better than dealing with "outsiders." This preference for dealing with "insiders" rather than "outsiders" was (and continues to be) widespread among managers in industrialized countries, including North America.

During the 1920s, employers quickly learned how to keep their authority and their ability to make unconstrained decisions intact despite the councils. Since very little changed inside the firm, many labor spokespersons considered the legislation a failure. Although they were supposed to create a form of industrial democracy, the new institutions were not strong enough to prevent many large companies from supporting the rise to power of the Nazi Party (Sturmthal 1944).

During the Nazi era, the entire system was dismantled. However, codetermination was re-established after the war. Initially, employees in the coal and steel industry were granted parity representation on supervisory boards.[3] Chairpersons were to be neutral outsiders who would break ties. And the labor side

---

3 German corporations today have both a supervisory board (which is roughly equivalent to a North American board of directors, although no top managers are permitted to sit on it and its main purpose is to develop broad policy guidelines) and a management board (comprising the company's top operating officers). The management board has collective authority equivalent to that of chief executive officers in North American corporations.

of the directing board would be able to designate one of the top corporate executives — the one with responsibility for human resources management. Many of these top management positions were filled by trade union activists who had previously served on works councils. The labor movement wanted this parity codetermination system extended to the whole of German industry, but management was opposed. Outside of coal and steel, as a result, the government re-established minority labor representation on directing boards. Employees were to elect a third of the board members, and the top executive corps was to be appointed by the board as a whole.

Labor was not satisfied with this situation. In the mid-1970s, it succeeded in having the law changed to require "near parity" in large corporations. Both employees and stockholders would elect half the supervisory board members, but there would be no neutral chairperson. Instead, the shareholder side would select a chair who, in the event of a tie, could cast a tie-breaking second vote.

Works councils, also re-established after World War II, had their powers strengthened considerably in 1972. The works councils now have codecision rights over a wide range of firm-level issues such as working hours, wage payment procedures, piece rates, individual employment contracts, the implementation of vocational training, job classification, and dismissals (both individual and mass). No decision can be taken unless the works council agrees. Deadlocks are generally settled by reference to binding arbitration, although few disputes require arbitration for their settlement (see Adams 1986). The councils are also entitled to economic information about the plans and prospects of the firm, but they have no codetermination rights with respect to corporate planning. In addition, they oversee the implementation of collective agreements and statutory requirements. The councils are not permitted to organize strikes. Most active works councilors are also trade unionists. The unions' extensive research and education facilities provide councilors with the skills required for responsibly and effectively carrying out their statutory duties.

Although this system was initially opposed by both labor and management, there is currently a very strong labor-management consensus that it has worked remarkably well (Thelen 1991; Freeman and Rogers 1993). It has allowed change to be introduced without major disruption. Employee representatives (both board members and councilors) must be informed about tentative plans well in advance of their implementation. Consequences of planned changes are discussed, and ways of dealing with them are built into implementation plans. Since consensus is sought before implementation, resistance subsequent to the change is minimized. Moreover, the decisions taken are widely considered to be better than they would have been without such broad-based input. There is general agreement that the requirement to consult and to reach consensus rather than submit disputes to third parties (who might very well hand down inappropriate decisions) has substantially modified managerial style. Traditionally, German culture elicited an authoritarian approach to employment relations.[4] The institutions of codetermination have resulted in a much more collaborative managerial approach. Employee representatives, on the other hand, have encountered first-hand the difficult and complex decisions continually facing management. This greater understanding has helped ensure more cooperation with and commitment to decisions taken.

In short, employees have gained because their interests are taken into account when critical enterprise decisions are under discussion and because there is a genuine effort to reach consensus regarding those decisions. Employers have gained because the quality of decisions has been enhanced, while resistance to change has been significantly reduced.

Employers feared that decisionmaking would be slowed down to the point of inefficiency. But generally that has not happened.

---

4 Employer authoritarianism is not, of course, uniquely German. Nevertheless, a strong historical pattern of vertical authority is considered a notable aspect of the German character. The fact that, historically and culturally, German employers were loath to share authority is pointed out here chiefly because their practice today is so notably contrary to that propensity.

Most employee representatives have been willing to defer to managers in areas beyond their expertise. Problems have occurred primarily where managers have failed to produce information needed to fully evaluate the results of proposed courses of action.

At one time, many viewed codetermination as a "fair-weather" system that would collapse in difficult times. Few still hold that view, because the system has functioned very well — even during the turbulent 1980s and early 1990s. Enormous restructuring and technological changes have taken place in many industries — for example, steel — with minimal disruption (Thelen 1987).

Pattern Bargaining

The Legien-Stinnes Accord encouraged the spread of multi-employer bargaining, which had begun to develop in a few industries before World War I. Union-management negotiations take place on a regional/industry basis. Although there is no national framework for bargaining, the system maintains coherence largely because of the effective domination of industrial relations by the labor market parties in the metalworking industry. Essentially, key agreements reached between the metalworkers' union and its employer association counterpart set a pattern for the rest of the economy (Soskice 1994).[5]

In practice, German labor accepts the basic principle that wage movements must stay within what is possible as a result of productivity increases and fully acknowledges the necessity of

---

5 To pay for the reunification of East and West Germany, the German government has assessed high surcharges. This approach has created an effective decrease in the purchasing power of German workers, who, in turn, have pressured their leaders to win higher wage increases. On the other side of the table, employers, including the government, have tried to hold the line on costs because of budgetary deficits in the public sector and enhanced international competition in the private sector. The resultant bargaining instability produced a number of uncharacteristic strikes in the early 1990s, spearheaded by unions other than IG Metall. The long-term implications of these developments are, of course, unpredictable at this time.

technological advance.[6] These attitudes are natural for a labor movement that considers itself (and is considered by others) to be the general voice of employee interests in the economy. German unions not only negotiate the sectoral interests of their own members but also represent the interests of working people as a whole. Collective agreements reached between unions and employer associations apply to approximately 90 percent of the labor force.

This broad bargaining coverage stems primarily from the fact that most employers belong to an employer association. Agreements, in effect, apply to all relevant employees of all employers in an association. Confronted with strong national unions, nonassociated employers stand to lose out (to be "whipsawed"). Thus, most employers join an association. In addition, there is a procedure (similar to one that operates in Quebec) whereby agreements may legally be extended to nonassociated employers. But it is not much used these days; the threat of extension is often enough to "encourage" all employers to associate.

Only 40 percent of German employees are union members, partly because nonmembers benefit from bargaining agreements as well. In North American terminology, they are "free riders." The right to join a union is sacrosanct in both law and practice. It would be considered highly improper for an employer to try to sway an employee's opinion on union membership. On the other hand, formal union security devices that compel reluctant individuals to be union members are considered equally unacceptable. Most workers join unions because of social pressure exerted by coworkers, who understand that unions need support if they are to carry out their functions effectively.[7] Workers also join because unions provide "conflict insurance" — that is, the union

---

6 According to Soskice (1994), they also fear that, if wages rise much faster than productivity, the central bank will intervene and raise interest rates, leading to a rise in unemployment.

7 Social pressure might also be looked at as a kind of coercion; it might then be argued that, if union activists are permitted to attempt to convince the nonunionist to join, employers ought to be permitted to attempt the opposite. North Americans, having generally accepted this argument, see nothing...

is prepared to intervene to help resolve any individual dispute. But most German unions, being poorly organized on the shop floor (Markovits 1986), have a difficult time putting a convincing case for union membership to the nonunionist.

Collective bargaining is highly regulated in Germany. For example, unions may strike and employers lock out only under very specific circumstances. All agreements are written. Disputes about the application of collective agreements or about rights stemming from statute and individual employment contracts are settled by labor courts.

Because of this structure, as well as the close (albeit informal) consultation between government policymakers and top business and union leaders, wage movements are usually coordinated with economic policy decisions. Considerable public debate takes place over economic forecasts and what wage movements the economy can afford in the context of these forecasts. With wage negotiations typically held annually, the result is a rational and responsive relationship between wage movements and economic policy.

The system also allows for the achievement of broad consensus over emerging policy issues. For example, there is broad agreement in Germany over the advisability of workplace-level restructuring in order to allow for more flexibility and worker commitment to continuous improvement in the quality and quantity of production.

Training and Education

Most Germans, along with foreign experts, view the training and education system as one of the most critical elements in the

Note 7 - cont'd.

...wrong in employers' expressing their views and preferences. In most European countries, however, the decision to join is generally considered to be between unions and employees. Because of the employer's position of power and self-interest, any employer involvement in the process is considered to be necessarily coercive and thus improper.

success of the German economy. German universities and institutes have very high standards, but the centerpiece of German training is the system of apprenticeship known as the "dual system."

At about age 15, German youngsters choose either to go on with academic education or to enter the apprenticeship system (Streeck et al. 1987). About half take the apprenticeship route. For the next three years (usually), they work in a firm under the close tutelage of skilled workers and trainers. They spend the equivalent of one or two days a week continuing their academic studies, and they attend technical classes during block release periods or during the evening. After three years, they take a comprehensive exam. Those who pass are declared prepared to accept difficult technical duties.

Many jobs in Germany can be carried out only by craftspersons who have completed the requirements of the apprenticeship system. Besides valuable skills, apprenticeship also encourages young people to acquire the mental habits associated with excellence.[8] The system is governed by a complex process (which has evolved piecemeal) in which labor, government (at both the federal and the state levels), and business all have roles critical to the effective operation of the overall system.

The federal government is responsible for labor market policy and thus for labor market training. The states, however, have constitutional responsibility for education and thus for "training" that takes place as part of overall education policy. Apprentices spend one or two days a week in state-provided classrooms, where they study both technical subjects and cultural subjects (such as German, history, and religion).

The in-company training is overseen by the Chamber of Commerce. Until 1969, in-firm training was entirely under the control of employers. Now, there are government-imposed regu-

---

8 Many of the observations made in this section are the result of interviews that I conducted with many of the principal actors in the German system in 1991 as part of a research project for the International Labour Organisation. Some of the results were reported in Wilson (1993).

lations regarding the content and structure of training. Regulations (as well as practically all aspects of labor market training policy) are established by the Federal Institute of Vocational Training, on which labor, management, the states, and the federal government each have an equal number of seats. Qualifying examinations are set by the Chamber of Commerce, but trade unions always have representation on the committees that set the exams. Chamber committees on which trade unionists have representation also approve the firms that do training within the dual system. Works councils have joint responsibility with management to oversee the training effort at the level of the firm. The number of training places and the specific content of the daily training schedule are issues for codetermination. The dual system thus requires quadripartite cooperation.

Another major characteristic of the dual system is the broad consensus over the need for employers to hire trainees during both good and bad economic periods. Apprentices are classified as students, not as workers, although they do receive a small salary (smaller than those accorded apprentices in most other advanced countries). This has been a key element in maintaining the effectiveness of the system through economic ups and downs. Continuity of the training effort has also been recognized as important to the operation of an effective training system by Canadian experts. But despite decades of almost continuous debate over training strategy, to date the parties have not reached agreement on instituting the principle. Instead, the intensity of training varies with the business cycle (Meltz 1990).[9]

---

9 One reviewer of this essay had the following comment: "This training system sounds extremely rigid. If the hallmark of the new economy is flexibility, doesn't the rigidity of its apprenticeship put Germany at risk? (By implication, should we imitate them if they are on the verge of becoming obsolete?)" The German experience suggests to me, however, that the current insistence on a dichotomy between regulation (bad) and deregulation (good) is bunk. It is not the extent of regulation but the form of regulation that is critical to economic performance. The German system is indeed rigid, but it is precisely this rigidity that ensures high participation and high-quality graduates. The British and US systems, which lack such firm controls and requirements, are much less successful (see especially Lynch 1994).

Japan

Socioeconomic Performance

During the past two decades, Japan's economy has continually grown at rates superior to those in the West, and the productivity of several of its export industries has surpassed western levels. Fifteen years ago, westerners wrote off Japanese production practices as a cultural oddity. Now, western firms are avidly attempting to emulate those aspects of Japanese practice that are compatible with western institutions (see, for example, Vogel 1979; Johnson 1988; Oliver and Wilkinson 1989; Womack, Jones, and Roos 1990; Adams 1991).

Besides growing dramatically, the Japanese economy has also provided full employment, low inflation, and a great deal of flexibility. Companies have been known to completely change product lines and markets in remarkably short periods of time. Japan also boasts a low level of strike activity, albeit a higher rate than that prevailing in northern Europe.

On the negative side, Japanese workers are said to suffer from considerable stress. They work much longer hours than do westerners and are under considerable pressure to produce. And Japan's social infrastructure is relatively underdeveloped by international standards. Until the oil crisis of the 1970s, Japanese government policy explicitly emphasized investment rather than social consumption. Improvements have since been made, but without reaching the level characteristic of Western Europe or North America.

Japan has devoted most of its energies to developing certain highly efficient and competitive export industries. It has been very successful in doing so. But domestic industries are less well developed in both efficiency and competitiveness.

While workers in the competitive export industries have high-level skills and high wages (indeed, the wages of Japan's industrial workers are now among the world's highest), their skills are very specific and may or may not be portable. Acquired through continuous training in specific firms, many may be of value only in that particular firm. This approach is almost the antithesis of that followed in Sweden and Germany, where the aim is to direct the movement of skills to those parts of the economy where they are most in demand. Because of "lifetime employment," the intense acculturation procedures of Japanese corporations, and the preference of firms for internally developed employees, interfirm labor mobility is very limited (Shirai 1983; Kuwahara 1987, 1990). On the other hand, the practice of training workers in a variety of skills gives them more mobility within individual enterprises than typical western firms offer.

Business-Labor-Government Relations

Although elements of the Japanese system may be traced back for centuries, the system as we know it today took firm shape only in the 1950s and 1960s. After World War II, the occupying powers encouraged unionization and collective bargaining, partly as insurance against the potential resurgence of a business-military elite like the one that drew Japan into World War II. By the early 1950s, virtually all major corporations were unionized and engaged in collective bargaining. The unions that emerged were enterprise based. All Toyota employees, white collar and blue collar alike, formed a single Toyota employees' union. Though national "federations" of employees in different industries were formed, the center of power remained at the local level (Levine 1958; Gordon 1985, 1990).

The 1940s and 1950s saw a good deal of industrial conflict in Japan. Unions wanted job security and egalitarian working conditions for their members. Management wanted the unfettered right to direct the production effort so as to be able to make the decisions necessary to re-establish the competitiveness of Japanese industry. Many companies were hurt by the strife, and more than one enterprise union was "busted." But out of the conflict emerged a general labor-management understanding. As had occurred earlier in Germany, a compromise was reached. Management would agree not to dismiss any "core" (regular, full-time) employees, and it would provide egalitarian conditions of employment (for example, all employees, from the highest-paid to the lowest-paid, would be entitled to participate on the same basis in the enterprise bonus scheme). Cafeterias, washrooms, parking lots, and so on, would all be used on an equal basis.

In return, employees were expected to devote their full capacities to the success of the enterprise. Regular employees were expected to continually improve their performance and that of their work group. They would be evaluated not only on their work but also on their "attitude" and their broader contribution to the performance of the enterprise. This undocumented agreement was, and remains, very informal. And though it varies in detail from company to company, its basic elements are so well known and deeply ingrained that they very nearly have the force of a constitutional principle.

Once this accord was reached, management set about leading Japanese industry on a quest that eventually resulted in its seriously challenging the dominance of the United States. Among the organizational techniques that became characteristic of the Japanese system were group work, continuous training, consultation, continuous improvement, lean production, and core periphery structures.

Group Work

Instead of dividing work into specific jobs, Japanese industrial firms typically assign substantial chunks of work to groups. Each group includes members with all the skills necessary to accomplish all the tasks required of it, including maintenance and troubleshooting. Because it is not specialized, the group is very flexible. Its pool of talent may be applied widely. Problems that arise are quickly diagnosed and addressed without the need to draw on specialists.

From the workers' perspective, the employment relationship is more interesting than in traditional western firms, where jobs and worker responsibilities are closely defined. Each day or week, something new is learned and some new challenge is addressed. The mind-numbing drudgery traditionally characteristic of factory work has given way, in the ideal Japanese factory, to the exhilaration felt by the members of a competitive sports team.

Continuous Training

Everyone in the group is supposed to be continuously learning new skills as well as teaching skills to less senior employees. Employees are evaluated on their performance at both learning and teaching. Many Japanese firms require new employees to spend several weeks or even months learning about the organization's history, philosophy, structure, and objectives. Since core employees are expected to spend a "lifetime" with the organization, employers do not fear losing their investment in training. Managerial experts consider firms with this kind of culture to have a significant advantage over those that are more static with respect to learning.

Continuous Consultation

Before critical decisions are made, including the strategic ones, a great deal of consultation takes place. The object is to reach an internal consensus. Ideally, no decision is taken unless all those who will be critically affected by it have a chance to consider and comment upon it. And ideally, if anyone (or any "actor" — for example, the union) objects strongly to a proposal, no action is taken until the objection is dealt with. In essence, this understanding provides the union with a veto; but that veto is rarely exercised.

The unions' general policy is that management should be accorded wide latitude to take decisions that support the best interests of the whole enterprise community. This attitude leads some western observers to conclude that Japanese unions are weak and management-dominated. But most Japanese and western experts would disagree. While considerable firm-to-firm variation naturally exists, Japanese unions generally fight hard for their members' interests, and disagreements — some leading to work stoppages — do occur. The apparently high level of cooperation and amicability seems to be due to the fact that Japanese management has lived up to its negotiated responsibility to take decisions in the best interests of all concerned, rather than to the unions' weakness or servility.

Continuous Improvement

As already noted, all employees are expected to contribute suggestions for improving productivity and quality. Formal "quality control circles" are often set up to make this process systematic. The ultimate object is total perfection and total flexibility. Ideally, every car built, for example, should be unique and defect free (Womack, Jones, and Roos 1990).

As productivity improvements are made, some workers naturally become redundant; this is why workers in many countries fear new initiatives and new technology. Few workers anywhere are willing to participate in a process that is likely to result in their dismissal. In Japan, the guarantee of "lifetime employment" overcomes this reluctance to participate in productivity enhancement. To management, the unions' insistence on guaranteed lifetime employment compelled great effort to make full use of every employee's inherent capabilities. Without the option of dismissal, Japanese managers were forced to explore creative human-resource solutions in order to be competitive.

Lean Production

Continuous improvement applied over several decades has resulted in very "lean" production systems. For example, Japanese factories carry very little inventory. The object is for each element in the production process to arrive "just in time" to be assembled. Lean production also implies, as noted earlier, that, as improvements in production are made, employees are removed from the production process. Operating with a minimal crew compels strict attention by crew members to the process and helps engender quality and continuous improvement. The process has been likened to lowering a river. As the water level is lowered, impediments to progress become apparent. When they are removed, the river is again lowered, repeating the cycle.[10]

Successful lean production requires employees who are highly competent and highly committed to improving the production process. This commitment is forthcoming in Japan partly because of job security but also because employees know that the financial results of productivity improvement will be equitably shared.

Core-Periphery Structure

Employees are prepared to continually contribute ideas for productive improvement because they know that

- they will not be dismissed as a consequence of more efficient practices, and
- they will participate equitably in the financial consequences of improved competitiveness.

But companies can make and keep such promises partly because of their propensity to hire part-time and limited-contract employees to whom such promises are not made. During ups and downs in business cycles and as the economy restructures, this "periph-

---

10 I am indebted to John Miltenberg for this imagery.

ery" may expand and contract. One problem with the Japanese system is that the benefits provided to "core" employees are not available to those on the periphery, the majority of whom are women. Still, full employment in the economy provides reasonable insurance that one's income stream will not be severely interrupted. Because of continual high demand, work is generally available for all who want it (Levine and Tyson 1990).

A Final Comment on the Japanese System

Oddly, as late as the 1970s, the Japanese did not view these practices as particularly effective (Kuwahara 1990). Japanese management longed to emulate US management and regretted the constraints under which it felt compelled to operate. Only in the late 1970s and early 1980s did the system's dynamics begin to be understood. Since then it has been widely emulated around the world. Recent research suggests that, in any part of the world, firms that successfully adopt these practices outcompete those that continue operating under older theories of labor management and production organization (Womack, Jones, and Roos 1990). Indeed, some business experts are convinced that these practices — or some close approximation to them — will become the norm by the twenty-first century. According to this school of thought, firms that do not embrace this system will fall by the wayside in the global competitive struggle.

Policy Consultation

Although the most innovative Japanese practices operate at the firm level, the total Japanese system comprises additional key elements. As in Germany, substantial consultation occurs at the national level, where efforts are made to reach business, labor and government consensus.

This process dates from the first oil shock of the early 1970s (Taira and Levine 1985; Kume 1988; Armstrong 1990). The shock caused negative growth and generated concern among all parties regarding continued economic progress. A government-convened series of tripartite meetings led to an understanding that has held more or less since.

Following the oil shock, unions pushed for large wage increases in order to track inflation; base rates increased by nearly 30 percent. Labor agreed to modify its wage demands, but only if government agreed to pursue fiscal and monetary policies aimed at moderating prices, attaining full employment, and expanding the social budget (then among the lowest in the developed countries). Business agreed to continue its commitment to lifetime employment for core employees and to institute adjustment programs where economic conditions made it impossible to honor that promise. Since then, labor-management consultation on various policy issues (for example, tax reform, working hours, social security, and employment equity) has expanded.

The need for effective labor-management relations is clearly understood in Japan. Business, labor, and government do not want to return to the turmoil of the 1950s. Indeed, that experience has produced a Japanese enterprise model that differs enormously from those operating in the West. Yasuo Kuwahara, a highly respected Japanese professor of industrial relations, has suggested that the Japanese enterprise should be thought of not as a vehicle for achieving shareholders' interests but rather as a "business community maintained by labor and management" (1990). In essence, the Japanese have put into effect the old North American cliché of the enterprise as "one big family." Becoming a core member of a Japanese corporation is much like becoming a citizen of a country, with all the rights and duties that such a status entails. By contrast, most Westerners still view the employment relationship as essentially a calculated market transaction in which money is exchanged for labor.

Bargaining Structure

As in North America, bargaining structure in Japan is decentralized. The most prevalent form of collective agreement has a single company and a single union as signatories. Unlike North America, however, labor and business organizations oversee Japanese bargaining. Each year, union-management wage bargaining takes place across the country, coordinated on the business side by the National Employers Federation (Nikkeiren) and on the labor side by Rengo, the major federation of trade unions.[11] Wage increases generally stay within 2 percent of the mean. The result is a rational and flexible response of wage movements to global developments (Soskice 1990).

Sweden

Socioeconomic Performance

Like Germany and Japan, Sweden has received considerable attention from economic and industrial relations policy analysts because of its socioeconomic success. As one US business consultant recently put it, "Sweden's achievements are beyond the dreams of most of the world" (Macoby 1991). Starting in the post–World War II period, and until very recently, Sweden was able to achieve, simultaneously and to a high degree, most of the socioeconomic objectives considered desirable by the advanced liberal democratic nations (Peterson 1985; Hammarström 1987). Until very recently, unemployment was continuously low. Even in the 1980s, when rates moved up to high levels in most industrialized countries, Sweden maintained full employment. It achieved a world-class economy based largely on the production of high-quality, high-value-added products that were marketed internationally. A very low level of industrial conflict was characteristic of the country from the 1930s to the 1980s. Sweden has one of the most extensive social benefit systems in the world. The services provided are regarded as being of very high quality, but they are

---

11 Rengo came into existence only in 1989, but the so-called spring wage offensive was coordinated before then by Rengo's predecessors.

also very expensive. In the 1980s, Sweden's tax rates were among the world's highest.

Despite their many accomplishments, the Swedes have had a difficult time controlling inflation. In order to keep their products internationally competitive, they have had to devalue the Swedish currency several times. Ensuring a steady flow of domestic investment has also been problematic.

Business-Labor-Government Relations

The December Compromise of 1906

In the 1890s and in the first decade of the twentieth century, Swedish workers began to organize in large numbers in trade unions. The official philosophy of the labor movement was a radical one. Like most labor movements in continental Europe, it wanted to replace capitalism with a more egalitarian socialist political economy. This goal aroused deep concern in the business community and the government. In 1902, feeling the pressure from both labor and government, business leaders formed a national association — the Swedish Employers Federation (SAF) — and opened up discussions with the major trade union federation, the LO.

The eventual result was the December Compromise. In essence, employers agreed to recognize the LO and its constituent unions as the legitimate voice for workers in general. They agreed to stop trying to dissuade employees from becoming union members. Employers also agreed to negotiate with the unions on an industry basis over wages, hours, and other basic conditions of employment. In turn, the employers insisted that the LO and its constituent unions agree to recognize the right of employers to "hire, fire, and direct work" as they saw fit, in order to organize production most efficiently and effectively. From the trade union perspective, the agreement was less than perfect. Still, the unions acquired general legitimacy. No longer would they have to fight for the right to exist and to play a constructive role in society. They also acquired a way (multi-employer bargaining) to be of value to a large number of working people.

Legislation in the 1920s and 1930s

In the 1920s and 1930s, legislation required that collective agreements last for a specific period of time and contain a peace obligation. According to this obligation, unions could not strike during the term of a collective agreement if a dispute arose regarding issues covered by the collective agreement. They could legally strike, however, if an impasse was reached over issues not included in the agreement. This system assumed continuous negotiations over new issues as they arose.

As a counterpart to the unions' right to strike, employers were accorded the right to lock out, a tactic they used often in the early decades of the twentieth century. A labor court was established to settle disputes over the interpretation of collective agreements and other legal and contractual conditions of employment.

Since employers did not feel obliged to recognize and negotiate with white-collar unions under the December Compromise, those unions lobbied government to pass a law requiring management to recognize and bargain with them. That law was passed in the mid-1930s. It requires employers, individually or through their association, to meet with and discuss disputed issues with any legitimately constituted union. Unlike North America, Sweden has no majority representation principle. Employers were expected to meet and attempt to reach agreement with unions that represented only a few of their employees. There was, however, no legal penalty for failure to agree.

Employers opposed the passage of this law, but quickly adjusted to it after it became an established fact. In fact, white-collar unions and employer associations had little difficulty arriving at a mutually satisfactory negotiating structure and process. By the 1950s, the large majority of white-collar workers

were covered by multi-employer collective agreements. Among
those involved in bargaining were middle-level managers, tech-
nicians, and professionals — employees often considered poor
candidates for collective action elsewhere (Adams 1975).

Today, almost everyone in Sweden (including about 70–80 percent of white-collar workers in private industry) is covered by a
collective agreement. In contrast to workers in Germany, almost
all those covered by collective agreements also belong to trade
unions — although, as in Germany, mandatory union membership is all but nonexistent. The difference is due to the fact that
the Swedes, unlike the Germans, have developed strong shop
floor union networks and thus are easily able to gain access to the
nonunionist. Moreover, the unions have secured the agreement
of employers to permit union organizing on company premises
and in the context of "processing in" new employees. The unions
also manage the unemployment insurance fund. One need not be
a union member to gain access to the system, but one must go to
a union office to fill out the paperwork.

The Saltsjöbaden Agreement of 1938

Despite the mutual recognition embodied in the December Compromise, Sweden witnessed much overt conflict during the first
three decades of the twentieth century. Recognition provided a
means for channeling conflict but did not put an end to confrontation. From the mid-1920s onward, successive governments
attempted to find a solution to the high levels of economic disruption. In the 1930s, a government commission recommended that,
unless the unions and the employers could find a way to resolve
their disputes without continual resort to conflict, which hurt not
only the economy as a whole but also third parties that had no
direct interest in the dispute, new restrictive legislation should
be introduced.

Neither labor nor business wanted to see new legislation. To
avoid that development, they held a series of meetings that

eventually produced a national conflict prevention scheme. It was named after the seaside resort near Stockholm where most of the meetings were held — Saltsjöbaden. Even more importantly, it produced an informal business-labor consensus to work together in the best interests of the economy as a whole and to respect each other's interests. After the Saltsjöbaden Agreement, Sweden had one of the lowest rates of overt industrial conflict in the world. In the past decade, however, conflict has again increased.

Centralization of Bargaining

During World War II, even though Sweden was not a combatant, it had to operate on a war footing. One result was pressure toward centralized wage setting. After the war, bargaining returned temporarily to the industry level. However, the 1950s saw the development of what might be called articulated bargaining.

In essence, bargaining took place at several levels. Every year or two, a national agreement on labor costs would be worked out. The deal would then be articulated, first at the industry level and then at the local level (company, plant, workshop, and even, in the case of white-collar employees in the private sector, individual). There was general agreement that wage movements should be closely correlated to the economy's productive capacity. To a large extent, national bargaining became an exercise aimed at achieving consensus on how much the economy could afford in the coming period. Even more than in Germany and Japan, this structure and process allowed for the achievement of national agreement on the direction of economic policy and on the relationship between government-administered fiscal and monetary policies and wage movements (Soskice 1990).

The Rehn-Meidner Model

Gösta Rehn and Rudolf Meidner, economists employed by the LO, developed a policy framework for the labor movement in the years after World War II. Their scheme included the following main elements (Meidner 1992):

- Under the *solidarity wages* system, workers doing equivalent jobs should be paid the same without regard to the employer's economic situation. Employers who could not pay the requisite wages should not be subsidized with substandard conditions but should instead free up capital to be invested more profitably and efficiently elsewhere.
- Unions should not oppose the introduction of new technology but should instead actively advocate its adoption.

The successful pursuit of these two objects would necessarily result in people being laid off, thereby threatening the union objective of stable employment and income. This problem would be solved by using *active labor market policy*. Laid-off workers would be guaranteed significant retraining and assistance in finding alternative work. In addition, the government would pursue fiscal and monetary policies resulting in full employment (Gross 1994).

There would be very little public ownership of productive organizations, but a fairly dense network of statutes and collective agreements would be created to ensure that business conducted itself in a manner deemed to be in the public interest.

There would also be a highly developed welfare state, providing universal economic and social security from cradle to grave. To win the support of the middle class, it would have to be of very high quality and thus would have to be expensive.

As well, a network of agencies, directed by representatives from labor and business (and other constituencies as relevant), would be created to manage the various aspects of social policy. For example, a Labor Market Board would have the responsibility for managing the active labor market policy. The trade unions would administer the unemployment insurance system.

Although the unions proposed this plan, it had considerable appeal for employers:

- Wages would be standardized and therefore removed from domestic competition — an object preferred not only by trade unions but also by employer organizations from early in the century.
- General wage movements should be largely predictable. (Contrary to expectations, however, wages tended to drift upward between wage rounds).[12]
- Technological innovation could be vigorously pursued with little concern for resistance to change.
- Profitable companies would have a high level of retained earnings available for reinvestment.

Because it had considerable advantages not only for labor and business but also for government and the citizenry as a whole, this scheme won very broad support. It functioned remarkably well for about three decades, during which Sweden attracted international acclaim for its "middle way" between the polar attractions of a state-controlled command economy and *laissez-faire* capitalism.

Contemporary Sweden

While these key elements of the Swedish system contributed to growth, stability, and equity for most of the post–World War II period, the system ran into trouble from about the middle 1970s

---

12 There are a number of causes of Swedish "wage drift." Bargaining establishes only the general amount by which the employer wage bill should increase. The understanding is that unions will not strike or otherwise exert industrial pressure to push wages over that general level. Nevertheless, in tight labor markets, employers have an incentive to increase employee income above negotiated levels in order to attract and hold valuable employees. Thus, wages drift upward as the result of the loosening of piece rate schemes, or the offering of high rates within established ranges to new hires, or increasing discretionary bonus and other incentive schemes. In other words, Swedish employers, sometimes in conjunction with local unions, find ways of increasing the take-home pay of the worker within the general negotiated agreement. The techniques are very similar to those used by Canadian employers to get around the restrictions of wage and price controls in the 1970s.

to the late 1970s and is currently in the midst of a crisis (Martin 1986; Ahlén 1989; Rehn and Viklund 1990; Kjellberg 1992). Several key factors seem to have caused problems for the system's operation.

Despite the December Compromise, unions continually attempted to influence the organization and management of the production process. By the 1950s, they had succeeded in establishing local union organizations responsible for overseeing and implementing collective agreements at the firm level and for working with management jointly to develop policy on specific issues. For example, national collective agreements had been signed during the 1940s calling for the joint regulation of health and safety and training at the enterprise level (Johnston 1962).

After World War II, the LO and the SAF negotiated an agreement calling for the establishment of works councils that would receive information on each firm's economic status and would jointly seek ways of achieving greater productivity.

Despite progress in expanding joint regulation at the enterprise level, the unions were not satisfied. The SAF continued to insist that the clause giving management the right to "hire, fire, and direct work" be included in every collective agreement. In the 1970s, the unions abandoned bargaining over the issue and were successful, working with the government, in pushing through a law requiring employers to negotiate about all issues of concern to workers. This law did away with the "reserved right" to "hire, fire, and direct work," specifying that management could no longer insist on including the clause in collective agreements.

Employers viewed this broad-ranging act as a betrayal of the spirit of the understanding, going back to the December Compromise, that they had the function of organizing and directing production. It also went against the implicit understanding, under the Saltsjöbaden Agreement, that labor and management should solve their problems without resorting to government intervention. On the other hand, trade unions felt compelled to seek legislation on these issues because negotiation had not produced acceptable results.

Business also opposed the development of more-detailed agreements at the central level (Myrdal 1991). Initially, central bargaining led to agreement on the percentage increase in the employer wage bill for the ensuing period. This "frame agreement" would be further articulated at the industrial and local levels. Thus, it seemingly provided both for national coordination of economic and wage policy and for sectoral and local flexibility. As bargaining rounds progressed, however, the LO began to press for special increases at the national level — covering, for example, women and low-paid workers. Thus, the central agreement became more complex. All employers in the SAF were required to put into effect a national formula.

In addition, the LO bargained successfully for decreasing differentials between highly paid and lower-paid employees. This change resulted in a more equal distribution of income, but also made it more difficult for employers to reward exceptional performance. Employers were increasingly unwilling to be bound to such constraints.

Labor felt that, despite considerable achievements on behalf of workers, "industrial democracy" had not yet been achieved. As a result, in the mid-1970s, the LO proposed (in addition to enhanced worker rights in the firm) the establishment of a wage earner fund. Companies with "excess profits" would have to pay a percentage of those profits into a fund controlled by worker representatives. Since payments would be made in shares rather than cash, capital would remain with firms and not be available for consumption.

While similar schemes designed to generate investment capital are relatively uncontroversial, the Swedish plan led to a great furor in the business community because it would pay no dividends and would not distribute its earnings or trade its shares. In short, whatever entered the fund would not leave. As a result, in the long run the fund would inevitably own the entire Swedish economy. Employers saw this proposal as an act of bad faith and delayed its introduction. A much-watered-down version of the scheme was finally initiated, but with a time limit that expired in 1990 (Pontusson and Kuruvilla 1992).

The Swedish system was also considered increasingly problematic by white-collar workers (particularly government employees). Until the 1980s, these employees generally deferred to the initiatives of the blue-collar federation, LO. An economic strategy worked out by the chief economists of the blue-collar federation (LO), the major white-collar federation (TCO), and the employer federation (SAF), specified that the wage agreements worked out in the internationally exposed goods sector should set the pace for the economy. This meant that white-collar and especially government workers were wage takers and that public sector incomes could not easily react appropriately to changes in the market. In the 1980s, public sector workers became increasingly less willing to accept these constraints. As a result, internecine conflict between unions increased.

The solidarity wages scheme also became problematic. It implied not only equal pay for equal work, but also the gradual narrowing of wage differentials. Workers with strong bargaining power thus had to agree voluntarily to accept wages and benefits below what their market power could achieve, so that weaker groups might improve their situation. Over time, that forbearance became increasingly difficult to maintain. In 1983, when the engineering industry employers' association sought negotiations separate from the national framework, the metalworkers union was not too difficult to convince.

In 1991, a Conservative government replaced the Social Democrats, and in January 1992 employers affiliated to the SAF withdrew from most bipartite and tripartite "corporatist" agencies. Because many major changes have occurred in recent years, it is not at all clear how the altered system is likely to function in future. In fact, speculation on the future of employment relations has become a major intellectual growth industry (see, for example, Kjellberg 1992). One thing, however, is clear: although no causal relationship may be attributed with certainty, the decline of consensus has definitely been accompanied by a deterioration of Swedish economic performance. Sweden's early 1990s recession was one of the worst experiences endured by any advanced industrialized country in recent decades.

The United States

Socioeconomic Performance

The United States still has the world's most productive economy but its lead over other advanced countries is now much narrower than it once was (Wheeler 1987; Weiler 1990; Neef and Kask 1991). In average standard of living, the United States ranks high in international comparison. Wealth and income, however, are distributed more unevenly there than in other advanced industrialized countries, and inequalities increased substantially in the 1980s (Reich 1992; Freeman 1995). While the United States has done relatively well in controlling inflation, it has achieved this goal primarily by permitting high rates of unemployment. For most years since World War II, US unemployment has exceeded the international norm. In the 1980s, however, US unemployment stayed at below-average rates, largely because of a social welfare system that provided benefits well below the international norm and that therefore required people to accept jobs below their productive potential and quite often below the poverty line (Rowthorn 1992; Wilensky 1992; Blank and Hanratty 1993). Finally, on average since 1970, the United States has lost two to five times as many days to industrial conflict as have countries with cooperative systems, despite the fact that a much smaller proportion of US workers are unionized than is true of the social partnership countries (see Table 1). During the 1980s, the rate of conflict fell substantially in comparison with the long-term mean and in tandem with a steep decline in union membership. Nevertheless, the rate was still nearly twice the mean for the cooperative group of countries.

Business-Labor-Government Relations

In all the countries considered here, animosity and confrontation characterized the early years of labor-management relations. In Japan, Germany, and Sweden labor and management were able to reach understandings that resulted in stable, productive, and collaborative relationships. But in the United States, aggravated hostility has been the dominant mode of labor-management interaction since the appearance of the first unions — and that hostility continues at very high levels today, though its overt expression in riots and violence is less evident.

Unlike their counterparts in Japan, Germany, and Sweden, labor, management, and the state in the United States have been unable to establish a framework of mutual recognition. For the most part, business and government have tried to exclude labor from participating in enterprise governance as well as in economic and social policymaking. Exceptions occurred during the two world wars, when US governments pursued consensus. There was also a short hiatus in antagonistic labor-management relations from about 1935 to 1948, starting before and extending beyond the war years. The governments in that period encouraged labor-management cooperation through collective bargaining. What might be characterized as a labor-management truce therefore held sway, although respect for the truce was less than universal. Starting in the 1950s, the system began to slip back into the confrontation mode.

Today, the system has bifurcated into two parts. In one, a few highly organized companies are attempting to move toward more cooperative relations with their unions in order to establish relations roughly similar to those found in Japan. A much larger group of companies, however, is engaged in actions apparently aimed at destroying the labor movement (Goldfield 1987; Adams 1989; Sexton 1991).

For example, many companies with long-term bargaining relationships have refused to recognize and negotiate with the relevant union in newly opened factories (Kochan, Katz, and

McKersie 1986). To keep unions out, illegal behavior such as firing those active in organizing campaigns has become rampant. The number of complaints involving dismissal for union activity brought before the National Labor Relations Board (NLRB) has increased dramatically since the 1950s (Weiler 1990). Three of four employers faced with a unionization campaign fight it vigorously (Bronfenbrenner 1994).

A "typical scenario" drawn from a study of 213 union organizing campaigns recently unfolded at Aero Metal Forms of Wichita, Kansas (Hurd and Uehlein 1994). When faced with a union organizing campaign,

> the company hired an attorney to design an antiunion campaign. Supervisors were trained to identify and combat union supporters, and captive audience meetings were held. Workers were warned that the union would take them out on strike and that they could be replaced; they also were threatened with plant closure. The two most vocal union supporters were fired. The April 22, 1991, election resulted in a 6–6 tie with three challenged ballots. By the time the NLRB reached a final decision and declared the union a 7–6 winner on April 5, 1993, only one union supporter still worked for Aero Metal. (p. 62).

Managers everywhere generally prefer to operate without constraint, just as unions prefer absolute job security for their members. When allowed to flourish, these tendencies have generally produced undesirable social and economic consequences. Recent US governments have permitted managers vigorously to pursue freedom from collectively negotiated constraints. Corporate leaders have no doubt been keen to do so because of substantial wage and benefit differentials between unionized and nonunionized firms. US unions have won premium conditions of work for their members compared to nonunion employees, and that success has given employers additional reason for wanting to operate "union free."[13]

Some of the key elements that have shaped the current situation are discussed below.

Pure and Simple Unionism

Unlike the labor movements in northern Europe, the mainstream of the US movement did not adopt a philosophy that called for major political change. The first successful trade union federation — the American Federation of Labor (AFL) — considered the unions' appropriate task to be winning job security, decent wages, and good working conditions for their own members by way of direct dealings with employers. The Federation consisted exclusively of craft unions and made little attempt to represent itself as the champion of all workers. It fully accepted the "free enterprise" system and thus did not pose a political threat to the fundamental principles of the political economy. As a result, unlike what occurred in Sweden and Germany, business did not consider its basic interests to be threatened and thus saw no need for a unitary response to the union threat (Adams 1982). Only modest, ineffective efforts were made toward business association for the purpose of dealing with industrial relations. Individual corporations worked out their own methods for addressing the challenge posed by specific unions.

A few attempts were made to achieve a national "basic agreement" like those reached in the other countries. Toward the end of World War I, for example, amid a global surge of labor militancy, a broad-based consensus emerged in the United States that workers should have in place some mechanism through which their collective interests at work could be represented to

---

13 That the impact of this variable is not determining is indicated by the fact that Canadian employers are not as aggressively anti-union as their US counterparts even though union/nonunion wage differentials are as large in Canada as they are in the United States. (See Riddell 1993.)

the employer. To meet that imperative, employers willingly offered to establish employee representation plans — an offer that the unions rejected in favor of strike-threat collective bargaining. In hopes of working out a compromise, Woodrow Wilson convened business and labor leaders nationally after the war, but those meetings collapsed in failure (Shuster 1990; Adams 1994a). The period from the late 1930s to the late 1940s may be thought of as one in which (similar to Japan currently) certain informal understandings were widely respected. An attempt to formalize these arrangements was made after World War II, but as with the attempt after World War I, it also failed (Dulles and Dubofsky 1984; Dubofsky 1994).

Decentralized Bargaining

The craft unions within the AFL prospered by developing strong internal bureaucracies, by negotiating written agreements (primarily at the enterprise level), and by vigilantly ensuring compliance with those agreements. Over time, as negotiations became regularized, local agreements expanded in size and in many specific situations began to encroach significantly on managerial functions. This union success strengthened the resolve of "nonunion" employers to maintain their status.

Since no national recognition agreement had been worked out, unions continued to try to organize on a plant-by-plant basis while employers generally continued to try to thwart union organizing drives. This continual opposition embedded a culture of confrontation. Even after recognition was granted in specific enterprises, the common managerial strategy was to minimize union influence rather than seek labor-management accord. As a result, bargaining rounds were typically characterized by confrontation. Rules of the game became established in which unions typically "demanded" much more than they hoped to settle for, and management generally "offered" much less than it was prepared eventually to agree to. Instead of continual negotiations, management's rights clauses in collective agreements gave management the "right" to do whatever it saw fit between bargaining rounds without consulting employee representatives.

In the 1930s, unionism spread to workers in the mass production industries. Although these unions were more political and egalitarian from their conception than were the craft unions, they generally followed the bargaining arrangements pioneered by the crafts. In addition to the aspects of bargaining noted above, a convention was established under which unions recognized management's right to organize the productive effort — meaning that the unions would not seek influence over technical, production, marketing, investment, and other financial decisions — in return for high wages, benefits, and job security based on seniority. The latter principle, in practice, implied a management right to lay off and rehire employees in response to economic circumstance.

Management's insistence on maintaining discretion over all issues not in the collective agreement led the unions to insist on increasingly elaborated agreements that, ironically, placed greater constraints on managerial discretion than in countries characterized by discussion about all issues of mutual concern as they arise.

The *Wagner Act* Model

The disputatious system just described was solidified with the passage in 1935 of the *National Labor Relations Act* (generally referred to as the *Wagner Act*, after its sponsor). The act's declared purpose was to encourage collective bargaining. Toward that end, it outlawed employer-initiated and -controlled employee representation plans. This action, designed to remove one of the blocks to collective bargaining, had the unintended effect of removing from employers the duty to consult with employee representatives where no union had been certified. Shortly after World War II, following the breakdown of the labor-management meeting convened by the Truman Administration, the *Wagner Act* was modified. Whereas the original act had forbidden employers to interfere with the right of their employees to join or form a union, the *Taft-Hartley Act* forbade unions to interfere with the right of employees *not* to join or form a union. *Taft-Hartley* also made clear that the duty not to interfere with employee choice did not mean that employers had to remain silent during union organizing campaigns. Although the National Labor Relations Board set up to administer the *Wagner Act* had forbidden employers to express any opinion about unionization (on the theory that anything the employer said would be interpreted as coercive by employees), the *Taft-Hartley Act* freed employers to express their opinions — including the opinion that employees would be better off without representation. In most subsequent union organizing campaigns, that point of view was vigorously expressed.

This stipulation relegitimized the rancorous opposition that had characterized labor-management relations prior to the mid-1930s. As a result, employer efforts to convince employees to forgo collective representation — behavior that would be considered contrary to minimally acceptable standards in Germany or Sweden, as well as contrary to the US consensus that had arisen after World War I — are now commonplace in the United States. Instead of encouraging consultation and joint regulation, the revised *Wagner Act* model perversely sets up a contest between unions and employers for "the hearts and minds" of the employees involved, thereby exacerbating confrontation (Adams 1993).

Failed Labor Law Reform in the 1970s

During the presidency of Jimmy Carter in the 1970s, a labor law reform bill was introduced into the US Congress. It would have speeded up union certification procedures and would have placed greater penalties on employers who broke the law. It easily passed in the House of Representatives and attracted a substantial majority in the Senate. However, a few senators engaged in a filibuster that would have required a large majority to override.

That majority could not be secured, and the bill died. A major reason for the bill's defeat was intense opposition by business. The episode widened the rift between labor and management (Kochan, Katz, and McKersie 1986; Lawler 1990).

Shortly after being elected president in 1980, Ronald Reagan was required to deal with a national strike by air traffic controllers. Instead of seeking an accommodation, he insisted that they all immediately return to work or face dismissal. Most did not return to work and were dismissed. Reagan may have been justified in doing what he did, because the strike was illegal. But his action was much stronger than that usually taken by government leaders in such situations. In fact, I can think of no other example where a class of workers was dismissed anywhere in the liberal democratic world during the past four decades for engaging in a strike, whether legal or illegal. US experts agree that the action was interpreted by business leaders to mean that the government was unlikely to interfere with their attempts to avoid or escape from the constraints of collective bargaining (Weiler 1990).

The Japanese Challenge

Starting around 1980, it became increasingly clear to decision-makers in the United States that US economic dominance was being seriously challenged from abroad. It also became more evident that "foreign" production and industrial relations methods were not idiosyncratic and culturally bound, but were instead very likely valid in many cultures (Levine and Tyson 1990). In short, foreign competitors, such as the Japanese, were not successful because of inherent cultural traits but rather because they were pursuing universal strategies that were superior to those of their competitors (Womack, Jones, and Roos 1990). This conclusion became unavoidable when Japanese firms operating in the West with western employees proved more productive than their competitors after effectively implementing the human resources and production systems first worked out in Japan (Kochan, Katz, and McKersie 1986; Womack, Jones, and Roos 1990; Adams, 1991).

US managers addressed the challenge using one of several strategies. Some went to their unions and insisted on a major overhaul of labor relations practices in order to implement schemes similar to those embraced so successfully by the Japanese but contrary to long-standing US practice. In many situations they met resistance from unions facing demands to abandon practices that they believed had served their members well for several decades. Despite this reticence, many unions went along with the new management proposals — at first because their political and economic weakness made it unlikely that resistance would be successful, and then because over time they became convinced that doing so was in their interests and the interests of the members (AFL-CIO 1994). Other employers opted for opening "nonunion" factories on greenfield sites and for pursuing policies designed to keep the union out, thus avoiding the burden of reaching accord with independent employee representatives.

The result of these developments is that consensual practices, processes, or institutions at the enterprise, sectoral, or national levels in the United States are at a premium. Some firms are trying to alter this situation by introducing various participatory schemes. But in general, those schemes depend on management good will for their existence and operational characteristics. They have not been set in place by statutory worker representation structures such as those in Germany and Sweden or by moral commitments as firm as those in Japan. As a result, their stability is questionable (Weiler 1990). Although there have been a few attempts to achieve labor-management cooperation on a regional or municipal basis, the general situation continues to be one of confrontation (Schuster 1990).

Implications for Canadian Public Policy

The experience of these countries suggests that the institutions of industrial relations are critical for socioeconomic success. Social partnership countries have outperformed adversarial countries by a substantial margin in recent decades, and there is every reason to believe that the margin will be extended in the next quarter of a century. The clear implication is that it would be wise for Canadian policymakers to find ways of moving Canadian industrial relations away from confrontation and toward consensus.

Although changing an employment relations system in fundamental ways is extremely difficult, the evidence reviewed here suggests that it can be done. Cultural and historical propensities and traditions are not determining. To achieve their current levels of social partnership, Germany, Japan, and Sweden all had to overcome deeply embedded cultural traits. There seems to be no convincing reason Canada cannot emulate that precedent.

Another clear lesson from the experience of these countries is that the short-term interests of labor and management may make it difficult for both groups to perceive and follow action that would serve their own long-term interests. The consensus arrangements achieved in Japan, Germany, and Sweden were entered into only reluctantly by labor, management, or both — and always under pressure from environmental events such as war, threatened revolution (Germany in 1918–19), threatened hyperinflation (Japan 1973), or the threat of government intervention (Sweden 1936). In many cases, governments actually had to intervene in order to set up participatory procedures (for example, works councils in Germany and workers' participation on boards of directors in Germany and Sweden). The apparent lesson for Canada? If substantial progress is to be made in re-engineering the industrial relations system, the primary onus for taking effective action rests on the shoulders of government. Furthermore, in carrying out that mission, government is likely to face considerable resistance from both business and labor because of their short-term interest in contemporary practice. A wealth of specific ideas on how to revise Canadian industrial relations is to be had from a careful review of the international experience. In other recent papers, I have outlined a number of specific recommendations for consideration (Adams 1993; 1994a; 1994b; 1995).

The evidence from these countries also suggests that institutions embedded in law are more stable than are informal understandings voluntarily entered into by labor and management. Although the Japanese understandings continue to hold, informal accords have collapsed in Sweden and the United States while legally based codetermination has survived and prospered in Germany (see especially Turner 1991).

The evidence reviewed here leads one to conclude that there is absolutely no relationship between the amount of labor regulation and economic success. The corollary is that labor market deregulation is unlikely to be an effective way of addressing international competitiveness. Instead, the challenge will be to devise institutional structures likely to elicit mutual efforts by labor and management in pursuit of continually improved efficiency and effectiveness. And that is unlikely to happen in a broad and sustained manner unless labor is given an effective voice in the making of all decisions critical to its welfare. One of Canada's greatest handicaps in the international economic arena is its exclusion of 60 percent of the labor force from the decisionmaking process. There can be no cooperation without participation, and there can be no participation without representation.

References

Adams, Roy J. 1975. *The Growth of White-Collar Unionism in Britain and Sweden: A Comparative Investigation*. Madison, Wisc.: Industrial Relations Research Institute.

———. 1982. "A Theory of Employer Attitudes and Behaviour Towards Trade Unions in Europe and North America." In K. Weiermair and G. Dlugos, eds., *Management under Differing Value Systems*. Berlin: deGruyter.

———. 1986. "Two Policy Approaches to Labour-Management Decision Making at the Level of the Enterprise." In W. Craig Riddell, ed., *Labour-Management Cooperation in Canada*. Toronto: University of Toronto Press.

————. 1989. "North American Industrial Relations: Divergent Trends in Canada and the United States." *International Labour Review* 128: 47–64.

————. 1991. *Employment Relations in an Era of Lean Production.* Faculty of Business Working Paper 361. Hamilton, McMaster University.

————. 1993. "The North American Model of Employee Representational Participation: A Hollow Mockery." *Comparative Labor Law Journal* 15 (Fall): 272–301.

————. 1994a. "Union Certification as an Instrument of Labor Policy: A Comparative Perspective." In Sheldon Friedman et al., eds., *Restoring the Promise of American Labor Law*. Ithaca, NY: ILR Press.

————. 1994b. "Labour Policy, Cooperation and Competitiveness: Recasting the Vital Links." *Policy Options* (March): 33–38.

————. 1995. *Industrial Relations under Liberal Democracy: North America in Comparative Perspective.* Columbia: University of South Carolina Press.

————, and C.H. Rummel. 1977. "Workers' Participation in West Germany: Impact on the Worker, the Enterprise and the Trade Union." *Industrial Relations Journal* 8: 4–22.

AFL-CIO. *See* American Federation of Labor and Congress of Industrial Organizations.

Ahlén, Kristina. 1989. "Swedish Collective Bargaining under Pressure: Inter-Union Rivalry and Incomes Policies." *British Journal of Industrial Relations* 27 (November): 330–346.

American Federation of Labor and Congress of Industrial Organizations. 1994. *The New American Workplace: A Labor Perspective*, A Report by the AFL-CIO Committee on the Evolution of Work, Washington: AFL-CIO.

Armstrong, Tim. 1990. "Industrial Relations: Japanese Style." *Challenges* (Winter) 1990, pp. 46–50.

Barber, C.L., and J. McCallum. 1982. *Controlling Inflation.* Toronto: Lorimer.

Berghahn, Volker R., and Detlev Karsten. 1987. *Industrial Relations in West Germany*. Oxford: Berg.

Blank, Rebecca M., and Maria J. Hanratty. 1987. "Responding to the Need: A Comparison of Social Safety Nets in Canada and the United

States." In D. Card and R. Freeman, eds., *Small Differences That Matter*. Chicago: University of Chicago Press.

Bronfenbrenner, Kate. 1994. "Employer Behavior in Certification Elections and First-Contract Campaigns: Implications for Labor Law Reform." In Sheldon Friedman et al., eds., *Restoring the Promise of American Labor Law*. Ithaca, NY: ILR Press.

Canadian Labour Market and Productivity Centre. 1993. *Canada: Meeting the Challenge of Change*. Ottawa.

Dodge, William, ed. 1978. *Consultation and Consensus: A New Era in Policy Formulation?* Ottawa: Conference Board of Canada.

Dubofsky, M. 1994. *The State and Labor in Modern America*. Chapel Hill: University of North Carolina Press.

Dulles, Foster Rhea, and Melvyn Dubofsky 1984. *Labor in America: A History*. 4th ed. Arlington Heights, Ill.: Harlan Davidson.

Freeman, R.B., ed. 1994. *Working under Different Rules*. New York: Russell Sage Foundation.

———, and J. Rogers. 1993. "Who Speaks for Us? Employee Representation in a Nonunion Labor Market." In B. Kaufman and M. Kleiner, eds., *Employee Representation, Alternatives and Future Directions*. Madison, Wisc.: Industrial Relations Research Institute.

Fuerstenberg, Friedrich. 1987. "The Federal Republic of Germany." In R.G. Bamber and R. Lansbury, eds., *International and Comparative Industrial Relations*. London: Allen and Unwin.

Goldfield, Michael. 1987. *The Decline of Organized Labor in the United States*. Chicago: University of Chicago Press.

Gordon, Andrew. 1985. *The Evolution of Labor Relations in Japan: Heavy Industry, 1853–1955*. Cambridge: Harvard University Press.

———. 1990. "Japanese Labor Relations during the Twentieth Century." *Journal of Labor Research* 11 (Summer): 239–252.

Grebing, Helga. 1969. *The History of the German Labour Movement*. London: Oswald Wolff.

Gross, Dominique M. 1994. "Unemployment and UI Schemes in Europe." In Christopher Green et al., *Unemployment Insurance: How to Make It Work*, The Social Policy Challenge 2. Toronto: C.D. Howe Institute.

Hammarström, Olle. 1987. "Sweden." In G. Bamber and R. Lansbury, eds., *International and Comparative Industrial Relations*. London: Allen and Unwin.

Helm, Jutta A. 1986. "Codetermination in West Germany: What Difference Has It Made?" *West European Politics* 9 (January): 32–53.

Hurd, Richard W., and Joseph B. Uehlein. 1994. "Patterned Responses to Organizing: Case Studies of the Union-Busting Convention." In Sheldon Friedman et al., eds., *Restoring the Promise of American Labor Law*. Ithaca, NY: ILR Press.

Johnson, Chalmers. 1988. Japanese-Style Management in America. *California Management Review* (Summer), pp. 35–45.

Johnston, T.L. 1962. *Collective Bargaining in Sweden*. Cambridge: Harvard University Press.

Kjellberg, Anders. 1992. "Sweden: Can the Model Survive?" In A. Ferner and R. Hyman, eds., *Industrial Relations in the New Europe*. Cambridge: Basil Blackwell.

Kochan, T.A., H.C. Katz, and R.B. McKersie. 1986. *The Transformation of American Industrial Relations*. New York: Basic Books.

Kume, Ikuo. 1988. "Changing Relations among the Government, Labor, and Business in Japan after the Oil Crisis." *International Organization* 42: 659–687.

Kuwahara, Yasuo. 1987. "Japan." In G. Bamber and R. Lansbury, eds., *International and Comparative Industrial Relations*. London: Allen and Unwin.

———. 1990. "Changing Industrial Relations in the Context of Industrial Restructuring: The Case of Japan." *Bulletin of Comparative Labour Relations* 20: 147–165.

Lacroix, R. 1986. "Strike Activity in Canada." In W. Craig Riddell, ed., *Canadian Labour Relations*. Toronto: University of Toronto Press.

Lawler, J. *Unionization and Deunionization*. Columbia: University of South Carolina Press.

Levine, David I., and Laura D'Andrea Tyson. 1990. "Participation, Productivity and the Firm's Environment." In Alan S. Blinder, ed., *Paying for Productivity*. Washington, DC: Brookings Institution.

Levine, Solomon. 1958. *Industrial Relations in Postwar Japan*. Champaign: University of Illinois Press.

Lynch, Lisa M., ed. 1994. *Training and the Private Sector: International Comparisons*. Chicago: University of Chicago Press.

Macoby, Michael. 1991. "Introduction: Why American Management Should Be Interested in Sweden." In M. Macoby, ed., *Sweden at the*

Edge: Lessons for American and Swedish Managers. Philadelphia: University of Pennsylvania Press.

Markovits, Andrei S. 1986. *The Politics of the West German Trade Unions*. Cambridge: Cambridge University Press.

Martin, Andrew. 1986. "The End of the 'Swedish Model'? Recent Developments in Swedish Industrial Relations." *Bulletin of Comparative Labour Relations* 16: 93–128.

Meidner, Rudolph. 1992. *The Swedish Model: Concept, Experiences, Perspectives*, Working Paper 1. Toronto: York University Centre for Research on Work and Society.

Meltz, Noah. 1990. "The Evolution of Worker Training: The Canadian Experience." In L. Ferman et al., eds., *New Developments in Worker Training: A Legacy for the 1990s*. Madison, Wisc.: Industrial Relations Research Association.

Myrdal, Hans-Göran. 1991. "The Hard Way from a Centralized to a Decentralized Industrial Relations System: The Case of Sweden and SAF." In O. Jacobi and D. Sadowski, eds., *Employers' Associations in Europe: Policy and Organization*. Baden-Baden: Nomos Verlag.

Neef, Arthur, and Christopher Kask. 1991. "Manufacturing Productivity and Labor Costs in 14 Countries." *Monthly Labor Review* 114 (December): 24–37.

Oliver, Nick, and Barry Wilkinson. 1989. "Japanese Manufacturing Techniques and Personnel and Industrial Relations Practice in Britain: Evidence and Implications." *British Journal of Industrial Relations* 27 (March): 73–91.

Ontario. 1984. Ministry of Labour. *The Search for Common Ground*. Toronto.

Peterson, Richard B. 1985. "Economic and Political Impacts on the Swedish Model of Industrial Relations." In Hervey Juris, Mark Thompson, and Wilbur Daniels, eds., *Industrial Relations in a Decade of Economic Change*. Madison, Wisc.: Industrial Relations Research Association.

Pontusson, Jonas, and Sarosh Kuruvilla. 1992. "Swedish Wage-Earner Funds: An Experiment in Economic Democracy." *Industrial and Labor Relations Review* 45 (July): 779–791.

Porter, Michael E. 1991. *Canada at the Crossroads*. Ottawa: Supply and Services Canada.

Reich, Robert B. 1992. *The Work of Nations*. New York: Vintage.

Rehn, Gösta, and Birger Viklund. 1990. "Changes in the Swedish Model." In Guido Baglioni and Colin Crouch, eds., *European Industrial Relations: The Challenge of Flexibility*. London: Sage.

Riddell, W. Craig, ed. 1986. *Labour-Management Cooperation in Canada*. Toronto: University of Toronto Press.

———. 1993. "Unionization in Canada and the United States." In D. Card and R. Freeman, eds., *Small Differences That Matter*. Chicago: University of Chicago Press.

Rowthorn, Bob. 1992. "Corporatism and Labour Market Performance." In J. Pekkarinen, M. Pohjola, and B. Rowthorn, eds., *Social Corporatism: A Superior Economic System?* Oxford: Clarendon Press.

Sexton, Patricia Cayo, 1991. *The War on Labor and the Left*. Boulder, Col.: Westview.

Shirai, Tashiro, ed. 1983. *Contemporary Industrial Relations in Japan*. Madison: University of Wisconsin Press.

Shuster, Michael. 1990. "Union-Management Cooperation." In J.A. Fossum, ed., *Employee and Labor Relations*. Washington, DC: Bureau of National Affairs.

Slomp, Hans. 1990. *Labor Relations in Europe: A History of Issues and Developments*. New York: Greenwood Press.

Soskice, David. 1990. "Wage Determination: The Changing Role of Institutions in Advanced Industrialized Countries." *Oxford Review of Economic Policy* 6 (Winter): 36–61.

———. 1994. "The German Wage Bargaining System." Paper presented at the Annual Meeting of the Industrial Relations Research Association, Boston, January. Forthcoming in proceedings. Madison, Wisc: Industrial Relations Research Association.

Streeck, W. 1984a. *Industrial Relations in West Germany: A Case Study of the Car Industry*. London: Heineman.

———. 1984b. "Co-determination: The Fourth Decade." In W. Wilpert, ed., *International Yearbook of Organizational Democracy*. Norfolk: John Wiley.

Streeck, Wolfgang, et al. 1987. *The Role of the Social Partners in Vocational Training in the Federal Republic of Germany*. Berlin: CEDEFOP.

Sturmthal, Adolf. 1944. *The Tragedy of European Labour*. London.

Taira, Koji, and Solomon B. Levine. 1985. "Japan's Industrial Relations: A Social Compact Emerges." In Hervey Juris, Mark Thompson, and Wilbur Daniels, eds., *Industrial Relations in a Decade of Economic Change*. Madison, Wisc.: Industrial Relations Research Association.

Thelen, Kathleen. 1987. "Codetermination and Industrial Adjustment in the German Steel Industry: A Comparative Interpretation." *California Management Review* 29 (Spring): 134–148.

———. 1991. *Union of Parts: Labor Politics in Postwar Germany*. Ithaca, NY: Cornell University Press.

Treu, Tiziano, ed. *Participation in Public Policy-Making*. Berlin: deGruyter.

Turner, Lowell. 1991. *Democracy at Work: Changing World Markets and the Future of Labor Unions*. Ithaca, NY: Cornell University Press.

United States. 1993. Department of Labor. *Report on High Performance Work Practices and Firm Performance*. Washington, DC: Bureau of National Affairs.

Vogel, E. 1979. *Japan as Number One*. Tokyo: Charles Tuttle.

Weiler, Paul C. 1990. *Governing the Workplace: The Future of Labor and Employment Law*. Cambridge: Harvard University Press.

Wheeler, Hoyt. 1990. "Management-Labour Relations in the USA." In G. Bamber and R. Lansbury, eds., *International and Comparative Industrial Relations*. London: Allen and Unwin.

Wilensky, Harold L. 1992. "The Great American Job Creation Machine in Comparative Perspective." *Industrial Relations* 31 (Fall): 473–488.

———. Forthcoming. *Tax and Spend: The Political Economy and Performance of 19 Rich Democracies*.

Wilson, David N. 1993. *The Effectiveness of National Training Boards*. Training Policy and Programme Development Branch Discussion Paper 110. Geneva: International Labour Organisation.

Womack, James P., Daniel T. Jones, and Daniel Roos. 1990. *The Machine That Changed the World*. New York: Maxwell Macmillan.

Inside the Black Box:
Human Resource Management and the Labor Market

Gordon Betcherman

Beneath the ebb and flow of the business cycle, unemployment has risen, more of it has become long term, job creation has tilted toward part-time and short-term arrangements, and earnings distributions have become more unequal.

These trends are clearly central to the current social policy debate on two counts. First, they have created substantial pressure on existing programs. The unemployment insurance (UI) and social assistance rolls have multiplied, leading to concerns about both welfare dependency and society's ability to pay. At the same time, difficult labor market conditions have underscored the limitations of our training and labor adjustment programs. Second, it is important to understand the role played by government interventions in determining the outcomes observed in the labor market. Taxes and transfers, insurance programs, and regulations all influence the behavior of individuals, employers, unions, and other institutions, and these influences need to be taken into account in proposing social policy reforms.

Although major differences clearly exist regarding the nature of appropriate reform, there is now widespread agreement that Canada's web of social and labor policies, largely designed in the 1960s, are not up to the challenges posed by the labor market of the 1990s and beyond. An effective framework will require an understanding of how public policy can best mix incentives with support to facilitate job creation, employability, and a feasible and politically acceptable level of economic security. This, in turn, will require some insight into how the labor market has changed and why it apparently has become a less dependable source of economic security for increasing numbers of Canadians.

The labor market trends catalogued at the outset undoubtedly reflect a host of social, cultural, demographic, and economic factors, and the complex interplay between them. In this essay, I contend that one important (and neglected) part of the story is taking place on the demand side, where workplace practices and, in particular, the evolving nature of "internal labor markets" (ILMs) are contributing to labor market insecurity and polarization.[1] Internal labor markets refer to the firm-level employment systems that govern the terms and conditions by which workers are employed and deployed. ILMs are shaped not only by the conventional economic forces of supply and demand, but also by institutions and laws, as well as strategic choices made by employers, employees, and unions.

Ultimately, the argument put forward here is that the ILM models most typical of Canadian firms lead to employment forms that, for substantial parts of the workforce, are based on low levels of commitment, short expected tenure, and little investment in human capital. These systems may well contribute, at least in the short run, to the flexibility that many employers are seeking. They also may serve the interests of a core of workers who are able to protect themselves through an "insider" status. However, these systems contribute to the polarization, contingency, job insecurity, and inadequate training that are now concerns for social policymakers. They "externalize" adjustment to change outside the firm and into the labor market where the costs are borne by those workers relegated to insecure, nonstandard jobs and by taxpayers who pay for an expensive social safety net.

---

[1] Part of the reason for this neglect is the lack of demand-side (establishment or enterprise) employment data, which operates as an important constraint on the questions labor market researchers can address. For a discussion, see Hamermesh (1994) and Osberg (1994).

This essay is organized into four sections. The first summarizes the major trends underlying growing employment insecurity in Canada. The discussion then turns to the internal labor market, profiling the practices within Canadian workplaces. The third section links the internal and external labor markets, considering how the dominant workplace models are contributing to the problems observed in the external market. In the final section, I argue that ILMs that generate greater investments in human resources and that "internalize" more of the inevitable adjustment to economic change within the firm could alleviate some of the pressures now felt in the external labor market. Selected policy options directed to this end are then discussed.

Labor Market Trends and Growing Economic Insecurity

A number of statistical trends suggest that economic insecurity has been on the rise for growing numbers of Canadian workers. Admittedly, this is a difficult conclusion to draw definitively because the available data cannot actually measure "insecurity" nor can they control for changes over time in the actual hardship created by a bout of unemployment, a spell of low earnings, or some other event.[2] Nonetheless, the trends reviewed in this section suggest some fundamental changes in the patterns of unemployment, employment, and earnings over the past two decades.

More Unemployment

Figure 1 traces out the unemployment rate in Canada over the postwar period. Underneath the cyclical fluctuations, there is a

---

2 For example, it has been argued that the increase in the unemployment rate over time must be interpreted with caution because the actual hardship of unemployment has been blunted by the rise of multiple workers within families and a stronger safety net.

Figure 1: *Unemployment Rate,*
Canada, 1946–93

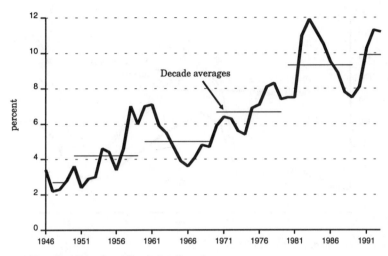

Source: Based on data from Statistics Canada.

clear ratcheting up of the rate over time. The horizontal lines drawn in the figure indicate average unemployment rates by decade; note the inching up of these averages and then the substantial increase for the post–1980 period.

An important question concerns trends in the unemployment rate for different segments of the adult population. In fact, rates have risen substantially for all groups, with particularly large increases among those traditionally considered to be "primary" earners. Taking 1975 as a base year, the upward trend in the unemployment rate has been more dramatic for males 25 years and older and for household heads than for the labor force as a whole (Figure 2). Certainly, the increased presence of multiple earners has eased the burden in some families when the primary earner becomes unemployed. However, it should be recognized that many families are still of the single-earner variety and that, where there are additional workers, they have relatively low average wages.

Figure 2: ***Unemployment Rate Indices,***
Selected Groups, Canada, 1975–93

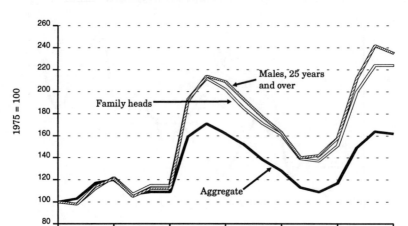

Source: Based on data from Statistics Canada.

Long-term unemployment[3] represents an aspect of the unemployment story with particular relevance to the social policy
debate. Admittedly, this has not been a problem here of the
magnitude that it has been in Europe.[4] Nonetheless, its importance has increased in Canada over the past two decades even
when one controls for overall employment conditions. This is
demonstrated by the outward movement of the spiral in Figure 3:
at a given level of labor market tightness (as indicated by the
aggregate unemployment rate), the proportion of total unemployment accounted for by long-term spells is now higher than was
the case in the past. In 1993, about 13 percent of the unemployed
remained so for at least a year (with over 30 percent out for

3 Long-term unemployment has two widely used definitions, one where the spell
 lasts at least six months, and the other where a 12-month minimum is used.
4 In 1992, for example, when 11.2 percent of the unemployed in Canada
 remained out of work for at least 12 months, the corresponding figure was
 42.2 percent in the European Union (OECD 1994). The severity of the long-
 term unemployment problem in Europe raises critical questions about its root
 causes and the effects of public policies and labor market institutions.

Figure 3: *Long-Term Unemployment Trends, Canada, 1976–93*

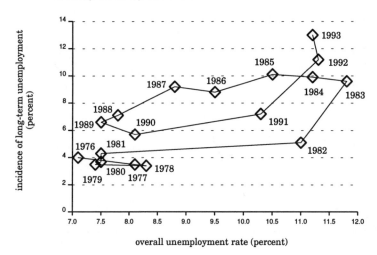

overall unemployment rate (percent)

Source: Based on data from Statistics Canada.

6 months or more). The long-term unemployment problem has become most serious for workers over 45 years of age and previously employed in declining sectors of the economy.

A Shift toward Nonstandard Employment

These unemployment statistics ignore the fact that job creation has been considerable in Canada over the past two decades. Since 1975, net employment growth has exceeded three million, which represents one of the better records among the industrialized countries. However, an important dimension of the economic security picture concerns the types of jobs that have been created.

In particular, "nonstandard" employment has accounted for much of the net increase in total employment. Nonstandard employment includes those workforms that depart from the traditional notion of a full-time, relatively permanent attachment to

Figure 4: *Nonstandard Employment as a Proportion of Total Employment, Canada, 1976–93*

Note: Nonstandard employment as defined here consists of part-time employment, short-tenure (full-time) employment, and independent contracting (full time, long term).

Source: Estimates by the author, based on data from Statistics Canada.

an employer. Using a definition that includes part-time, short-term (employed for less than six months), and temporary-help work, as well as independent contractors (the self-employed without any employees), nonstandard employment now represents nearly 30 percent of total employment (Figure 4).[5] Much of this employment (although not all) is relatively poorly paid, provides few benefits, rarely includes training or advancement opportunities, and the jobs themselves are, by their very nature, insecure (Economic Council of Canada 1990, 1991).

---

5 It is difficult to construct a time series on nonstandard employment that predates the 1970s, primarily because of a lack of data on short-term, temporary help, and independent contract employment. However, a long time series does exist on part-time work, the largest single component of nonstandard employment. In 1953, part-time work accounted for 3.8 percent of total employment, compared with 17.3 percent in 1993. This suggest that all nonstandard work probably accounted for less than 10 percent of total employment at that time.

The importance of the growth of nonstandard work to the social policy debate depends on what is driving the phenomenon. Certainly, these arrangements suit some people because they allow employment to be combined with other endeavors, such as education or household-related activities. In this sense, then, the proliferation of nonstandard workforms has made labor force participation more accessible than was the case in earlier times. Nonetheless, as we will see later in this essay, an important reason for their proliferation appears to be a growing preference on the part of many employers to structure jobs along nonstandard lines, typically to enhance flexibility or to reduce costs. As a result, increasing numbers of workers are in these types of employment — and experiencing the attendant insecurity — because they cannot find full-time, more permanent positions.

Changes in the Distribution of Earnings

Over the past two decades, the distribution of earnings has become more unequal and polarized. Table 1 illustrates these trends using the Gini coefficient to measure inequality and using the proportion of workers earning between 75 and 150 percent of the median as an indicator of polarization.[6] In a recent analysis, Morissette, Myles, and Picot (1993) verify the growth in inequality and the polarization, employing a wide range of measures which are sensitive to different aspects of distributional changes.

While the earnings distribution has clearly shifted, obviously the nature of the shift is important in assessing its social significance. For example, growing inequality could reflect income gains at the upper end of the distribution, with no worsening

---

6 The Gini coefficient ranges between 0, where incomes are equally distributed across a population, and 1, where all of the income is held by one person (or family). It should be noted that polarization refers to a slightly different concept than inequality — that is, a shift away from the middle and toward the high and low ends of the distribution.

Table 1:   *Earnings Inequality and*
            Polarization, Canada, 1967–91

	Gini Coefficient	Proportion of Workers Earning between 75 and 150% of Median
1967	0.363	0.42
1973	0.379	0.37
1981	0.378	0.36
1986	0.396	0.32
1988	0.396	0.32
1990	0.398	0.34
1991	0.403	0.32

Note: Based on annual earnings of workers aged 18 to 64 earning at least 5 percent of national annual average.

Source: Data from Statistics Canada.

at the lower end; similarly, polarization could be observed if no other changes occurred other than previously middle-level earners moving up to high-income categories. The Morissette, Myles, and Picot study demonstrates, however, that the distributional shifts have not been so benign. They find that an important part of the story has been sizable relative earnings declines at the bottom end of the distribution as well as a "declining middle" that has shifted downward as much as upward.

For men, real annual earnings for the bottom quintile (fifth) decreased by 16.3 percent between 1973 and 1989 while, at the same time, they increased by 7.9 percent for the upper quintile.[7] Over the same period, the proportion of the male workforce with

7 Over the same period among full-time, full-year male earners, Morissette, Myles, and Picot find that earnings of those in the bottom quintile fell by 7.6 percent while those in the upper quintile experienced earnings gains of 9 percent.

"middle-level" earnings shrank by 9.1 percent, with 4.2 percent falling down into the low category and 4.9 percent rising upward.[8]

These scenarios also apply to women working on a full-time, full-year basis (but not as strongly when the complete population of female workers is included).[9] The female inequality trend includes particularly strong growth between 1973 and 1989 in the top quintile (of 26 percent) at the same time that real earnings were declining (by 3 percent) for the bottom quintile. In terms of polarization, the proportion of women with middle-level earnings fell by 7.7 percent, with 5.3 percent slipping into the bottom earnings classes and 2.4 percent moving up.

The bottom line is that economic insecurity stemming from the labor market not only appears to be growing but is also becoming more unequally distributed. While workers with a high degree of skills or experience are not immune from insecurity, they are much more able than their less skilled or experienced counterparts to protect themselves.

Indeed, the Morissette, Myles, and Picot analysis underlines the importance of experience in explaining the inequality and polarization trends in Canada. The returns to experience have increased significantly since the early 1980s, with the result that the wages of young people relative to other workers have declined dramatically. Given the fall in the relative supply of young workers, it is difficult to account for this without turning to political or institutional factors. This brings us to the workplace and the role of internal labor markets in explaining some of the trends identified in this section.

8 This calculation is based on a classification of earnings into ten categories, with boundaries selected so that, in the base year, each included approximately 10 percent of all earners. Using the same real boundaries for 1989, Morissette, Myles, and Picot then allocate the workforce in that year accordingly. The trends cited in the text are based on classifying the middle six categories as middle earnings, with the lower and upper groups consisting of those in the bottom two and top two earnings categories, respectively.

9 For the female labor force as a whole, Morissette, Myles, and Picot find little evidence of growing inequality or polarization because major increases in the hours worked by part-time/part-year women have led to substantial earnings gains at the lower end of the distribution.

Trends in Internal Labor Markets

Internal labor markets remain something of a "black box" to Canadian researchers. Little has been written on prevailing workplace practices or their impacts on the labor market. In this section, I review new evidence on Canadian workplace practices in order to summarize internal labor market trends in this country.[10] In the next section, the links between these internal labor markets and the external market are considered.

Established ILM Models and the Pressures for Change

Internal labor markets refer to the set of administrative rules, procedures, and policies within firms that regulate the definition of jobs, the deployment of labor, compensation, and employment security. Together, these determine the pricing and allocation of workers, as well as the governance of the workplace (Doeringer and Piore 1971). While the features of the internal labor market will reflect the reality of the "external" market, the significance of the ILM concept rests with the proposition that what happens within the firm matters a great deal as well.

Osterman (1988) has traced the emergence of the internal labor market models that have dominated North American workplaces during much of the post–World War II period.[11] Actually, two types of systems have been characteristic — one for white-collar employees and the other for blue-collar workers. The inter-

---

10 This evidence comes from a two-year project on Canadian human resource management trends carried out under the auspices of the Queen's University Industrial Relations Centre. One of the major datasets for the project, the Human Resource Practices Survey, is the source of most of the empirical results reported in this section of the essay. For the final report of the project on human resource management trends, see Betcherman et al. (1994).

11 While Osterman's treatment focuses on US workplaces, the historical evolution of ILMs applies to Canada as well. An important question concerns whether there are still North American models, or whether Canada and the United States have diverged.

esting thing about these models is how each, *as a system*, has addressed the conflicting interests of management and labor — essentially the former's need for flexibility and the latter's requirement for security. While the nature of the blue- and white-collar models differs a great deal, for decades each represented a workable set of tradeoffs.

The blue-collar (or "job control") system typically has applied in union settings, although there has been considerable imitation in the non-union sector as well. The prototype includes tight job definitions and work rules, seniority-based deployment, wages based on the job rather than the worker, and no formal job security (but predictable risk through layoffs according to reverse seniority). For management, this model has offered broad prerogative over production decisions as well as the freedom to adjust the size of the workforce as required. However, this flexibility is constrained by the formal rules and procedures that regulate how work is organized and eliminate managerial arbitrariness in determining how labor is allocated. As Osterman (1988) has put it, the value of the system for workers is in "creating security in the face of an insecure environment" (p. 65).

The white-collar model has typically applied to professional, technical, and administrative work in non-union settings. Unlike the blue-collar system, it has been based on broad and fluid job definitions, assignment and compensation based on merit, and a commitment (either implicit or explicit) to job security. The white-collar model provides a high degree of operational flexibility to management in terms of organizing work and using its workforce. It also presumes substantial commitment on the part of employees to the organization. The job security pledge is labor's *quid pro quo* for this commitment and for accepting the flexibility-related demands of the model.

Beginning in the late 1970s and early 1980s, pressure started building on these established systems. Growing competition (both domestic and offshore) has posed the most serious challenge. As competitive pressures heightened, employers first became dissat-

isfied with the blue-collar model and the inefficiencies and inflexibilities that had built up through the accumulation of the
formal rules and procedures regulating that system.

Technological change added to the pressures. The widespread diffusion of microelectronics called into question the Taylorist principles of production that have been so closely tied to the
job-control ILM model.[12] The potential of computer-based production could only be fully exploited through flexible specialization
— and not Taylor's scientific management — which required far
less rigid workplace practices than were typical of the traditional
blue-collar system.

On the other hand, the white-collar model offered management much of the operational flexibility that it was looking for in
the new environment. Accordingly, that system did not come
under the same challenge in the 1980s. However, as competitive
pressures and difficult business conditions persisted and even intensified into this decade, employers started to weaken and even
back off from their commitment to the job security pledge. And, since
this pledge was so fundamental to the white-collar bargain, this
inevitably has jeopardized the stability of the model itself.

Internal Labor Markets in Canadian Industry

How have Canadian firms responded on the human resource
front to the intensified competition, the new technologies, and
other environmental pressures? To address this question, my
colleagues and I conducted the Human Resource Practices Survey
(HRPS) in 1993. The HRPS sample includes 714 establishments

---

12 The model was named after Frederick Winslow Taylor, an American engineer
whose ideas in the early decades of this century have formed the dominant
production methods in the United States and elsewhere. "Taylorist" methods
were based on a carefully conceived division of the production process into
narrow, repetitive tasks, with close supervision at all stages.

from across the country in four broad and diverse sectors: wood products, fabricated metal products, electrical and electronic products, and a selection of business services. While these sectors were chosen to reflect a wide range of industries in the Canadian economy, the survey does not cover the public, quasi-public, or traditional services sectors (for example, trade and consumer services). The sample also underrepresents small establishments.[13]

The HRPS gathered data on the organizational "environment" (for example, market conditions and technological change), business strategy, various establishment performance measures, as well as practices in a number of areas relevant to the internal labor market. These include employment structure, recruitment and selection, job design, training, employee participation, and compensation.

Using a statistical technique called "cluster analysis" on the practices reported by the respondents in these and other human resource areas, we identified three distinct internal labor market types among the HRPS establishments.[14]

The first system, which we call *traditional*, includes firms with ILMs based on a low degree of commitment between workers and the employer and low levels of investment in the workforce. Organizations in this cluster are characterized by: conventional (that is, Taylorist) job designs; limited employee participation in the operation of the work unit or organization; "straight" compensation systems (that is, without incentive-based features); little or no training; no flexible scheduling arrangements; and little integration of human resource issues in overall business planning. Establishments fitting into the traditional cluster were

---

13 For more details on the HRPS, see Betcherman et al. (1994).

14 Cluster analysis is a statistical technique that assigns data observations to clusters such that the variation within clusters is minimized while the variation among clusters is maximized. For more details on the application of cluster analysis to the HRPS sample and on the clusters described below, see Leckie (1994).

disproportionately in wood and fabricated metal products and in the small-firm-size categories (less than 100 employees).

In effect, firms fitting into the traditional model do not see human resources as a decisive competitive factor and, as a consequence, do not invest in ILM systems designed to enhance workforce skills and commitment. In contrast, firms in the other two clusters do view human resources as a key to competitiveness and the nature of their internal labor markets reflects this.[15] While each includes features meant to develop and tap labor's productive capabilities, these two models differ in terms of the specific practices that are emphasized.

One, labeled *compensation-based*, focuses on extrinsic rewards to create the productivity incentives. Firms fitting into this model typically report sophisticated compensation systems including above-market wages, extensive benefits, and variable, or incentive, pay schemes. They also tend to be characterized by strong ILM "ladders," with promotion from within and an emphasis on training. Large establishments (over 250 employees) and those in business services were overrepresented in the compensation-based cluster.

The other, which we call *participation-based*, emphasizes the quality of work and intrinsic rewards to motivate employees. Firms fitting into this system have a high incidence of employee participation (through formal programs such as labor-management committees, employee involvement, problem-solving groups, and so on). They also focus on enhancing job design (for example, job enrichment/rotation and/or teams) and invest considerably in training. Establishments in the mid-size class (100–249 employees) and in the electrical and electronic products sector were disproportionately represented in the participation-based cluster. So, too, were firms reporting significant technologi-

---

15 The HRPS data do indicate differences across clusters in terms of the strategic importance assigned to human resources within the overall business plan. See Betcherman et al. (1994) and Leckie (1994).

cal change and reorganization of the work process over the preceding five-year period.

Figure 5 shows how the HRPS sample fits into these three ILM groups. As panel (a) indicates, the traditional model describes slightly more than one-half of the respondents (53 percent), with the remainder relatively evenly split between the participation- and compensation-based systems.

While panel (a) demonstrates the prevalence of the traditional model, it actually understates the degree to which that system is dominant within the sectors surveyed. The reason for this is that small establishments — a group underrepresented in the HRPS sample — have a strong propensity toward traditional ILMs. For example, 70 percent of the HRPS respondents with fewer than 50 employees fit into the traditional cluster, compared with 18 percent of those with at least 250 employees. Panel (b) presents an adjusted distribution after weighting the HRPS sample so that it reflects the actual (that is, real economy) establishment size distributions of the four sectors surveyed.[16] As expected, this adjustment results in an even stronger presence for the traditional system (70 percent), with the participation- and compensation-based models accounting for just 18 and 12 percent, respectively.

The third chart in the figure captures another aspect of the distribution — that is, the proportion of employees working in each of the different ILM types (panel [c]). This distribution, based on the weighted sample used in panel (b), incorporates the fact that, on average, fewer people work in a traditional ILM establishment than in one characterized by either of the other two systems. From the perspective of numbers of employees (rather than establishments), then, the traditional model is not as dominant. Nevertheless, we estimate that it represents the employment system for the majority of the workforce (54 percent) in the sectors surveyed.

---

[16] For more details, see Leckie (1994).

Figure 5: *Distribution of Establishments and Employees, HRM Clusters*

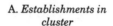

A. *Establishments in cluster*

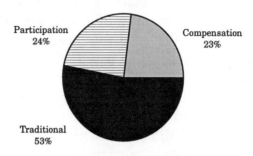

Participation
24%

Compensation
23%

Traditional
53%

B. *Establishments in cluster after weighting*[a]

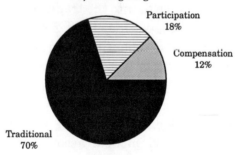

Participation
18%

Compensation
12%

Traditional
70%

C. *Employees in cluster after weighting*

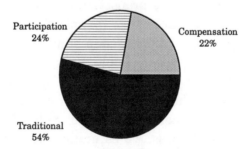

Participation
24%

Compensation
22%

Traditional
54%

[a] The sample results were weighted using Statistics Canada establishment-count data on establishment size (number of employees) in each of the four sectors that were surveyed for the HRPS.

Source: Betcherman et al. 1994, based on data from the Human Resource Practices Survey.

Linking the Internal
and External Labor Markets

There is now a widespread belief that human resources are a key, if not *the* key, to success in today's competitive, high-technology business environment. However, the picture of internal labor markets described by the HRPS is quite different. While there are exceptions, most establishments (employing more than half of the workforce) have what we have termed "traditional" employment systems characterized by low levels of human capital investment, Taylorist forms of work organization, conventional (that is, limited) modes of employee involvement, and compensation systems that do not create incentives for skills acquisition or high performance.

Clearly, one must be careful about generalizing from the Human Resource Practices Survey about the state of Canadian internal labor markets. Most obviously, the focus of the HRPS on four sectors leaves much of the economy uncovered. However, the sectors included are broad, and they represent significant components of the overall industrial structure (that is, the resource sector; traditional manufacturing; high-tech, high value-added manufacturing; and dynamic, producer services). If anything, one might expect the excluded sectors (such as government, trade, and consumer services) to exhibit largely traditional ILM patterns.

In this section, I turn to the implications of Canadian ILM patterns — and, particularly, the dominance of the traditional model — for four key labor market issues: job security, nonstandard employment, training, and polarization. An important theme running through the discussion is the relevance of what takes place in internal labor markets for the external market.

Job Security

Figure 6 compares countries along two dimensions of job stability — short-tenure employment (that is, less than one year) and

Figure 6: *Job Stability in Canada and*
Other OECD Countries, 1991

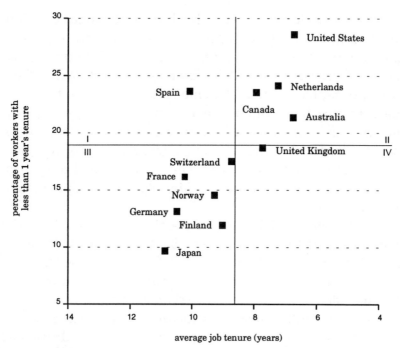

average job tenure (years)

Source: OECD 1993, 133.

average tenure. Movement from bottom to top and from left to right signifies increasingly unstable employment patterns. As Figure 6 indicates, substantial differences exist across countries in terms of job tenure and job security. For the most part, the European countries are in the lower-left quadrant where employment tends to be stable, while the United States and Canada are in the upper right, where employment is more unstable.

According to the Organisation for Economic Co-operation and Development (OECD 1993), the differences shown in Figure 6 cannot be explained by demographic factors such as the age and sex composition of national labor forces; nor are they due to variations across countries in the industrial makeup of employment. This suggests that the important variables are institutional. Societies can develop very different institutional arrangements to govern the employment relationship, the nature of the workplace, and to define the roles and responsibilities of the state and the private sector. The European and North American cases provide a sharp contrast in these institutional arrangements, with very different labor market implications.

By and large, countries in the lower-left quadrant have social and labor policies and workplace institutions that foster relatively high degrees of commitment between employer and employee. This set of arrangements has some obvious advantages. For example, those employed are likely to have job security and there is relatively little contingent, poorly paid employment. Clearly, there are disadvantages as well that stem from various inflexibilities in these labor markets. These include high levels of unemployment, much of it long-term, and poor records of job creation.

In contrast, countries in the upper-right quadrant, including the United States and Canada, are characterized by institutional arrangements — both within the workplace and at the level of public policy — that do not support a strong commitment between employer and employee. As we have already seen, most firms surveyed in our research follow a traditional ILM model that is not designed to encourage that sort of employment relationship. It should be noted that there are clear benefits stemming from the flexibility inherent in these systems. Compared to the European experience, job creation has been healthy in North America and unemployment (or at least long-term unemployment in the Canadian case) has been far less severe.

However, these ILM systems can cause various problems for the external labor market. The low level of commitment and the limited investments in employees do not create incentives for firms to adjust internally to changes in labor demand due to a business downturn or technological change. More typically, these firms rely on layoffs, which places virtually all of the adjustment pressures on the external labor market. This externalization of the adjustment process is abetted by public policy, most notably the UI system, which places no extra costs on firms that download adjustment on the labor market. These ILM systems also generate little workplace training, as I will discuss below. As a result, workers tend not to have had the opportunity to enhance their employability and, therefore, their re-employment chances after being laid off.

Nonstandard Employment

Another aspect of the job security issue concerns the proliferation of nonstandard employment. As we saw earlier (Figure 4), the share of jobs that are part time, short term, or temporary in nature has increased considerably over the past 15 years. These jobs, virtually by definition, are unstable. Compared to full-time, more permanent employment, they do not have the expected tenure, wages, or benefits (such as employer pension coverage) necessary to offer either short-term or long-term economic security (Economic Council of Canada 1990, 1991). Where that security cannot come from other private sources — that is, other family members — the burden to provide it will ultimately fall on social programs.

The policy implications of the growth in nonstandard employment depend very much on why this is happening. If it is due to the preferences of increasing numbers of individuals for those forms of work, the trend obviously raises fewer social concerns than if it is being driven by other forces, such as a growing employer preference for replacing standard jobs with nonstandard ones.

Unfortunately, this is a difficult issue to address empirically. In the first place, the distinction between "voluntary" and "involuntary" nonstandard employment (that is, from the perspective of the employee) is not always clear.[17] Nor is there much quantitative information to apply to the problem.

One relevant source of data is the time series on involuntary part-time employment, which measures the percentage of part-time workers indicating they are in those jobs because they cannot find full-time work. In general, this involuntary share moves up and down with the labor market conditions. This can be seen from Figure 7, which tracks the involuntary share along with the aggregate unemployment rate. However, Figure 7 also shows that, underneath the cyclical fluctuations, there has been an upward trend in the amount of part-time work recorded as involuntary. In 1993, for example, the involuntary share of part-time employment reached 35.5 percent, which is more than 5 points higher than the share reached during the early 1980s, when the unemployment rate was at similar levels.

If one accepts that Figure 7 indeed captures a valid trend toward more "involuntary" nonstandard employment, a range of possible explanations exists. One driving force could be increasing numbers of individuals from the traditional pool of nonstandard workers wanting to work in standard jobs. This could be due, for example, to the rising incidence of single-parent families, which would induce those (largely female) who historically would have been nonparticipants in the labor force or secondary earners to assume primary earner roles. It could also be due to the increasing polarization in the labor market and to the incentives that creates to "outsiders" to share in the compensation and security benefits associated with full-time, standard employment status (that is, employment in the "good jobs" sector). While these

---

17 That is, preferences are not completely exogenous but are formed on the basis of the prevailing context. An individual who reports working in a nonstandard job on a "voluntary" basis could be making that judgment knowing, for example, that child care support is not available for a job that requires more time or commitment. Similarly, someone reporting "involuntary" nonstandard employment (that is, a standard job was not available) could have engaged in only a very limited job search. In each of these cases, then, it could be argued that the voluntary/involuntary designation is not completely accurate.

Figure 7: *Involuntary Part-Time Employment and*
Aggregate Unemployment, Canada, 1975–93

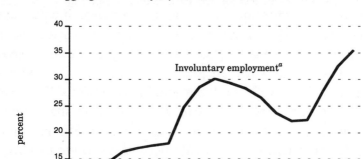

Source: Based on data from Statistics Canada.

a as a percentage of total part-time employment.

hypotheses seem plausible, there have been few, if any, serious attempts to assess their validity.

The apparent rise in involuntary nonstandard work could also reflect an increasing preference on the part of employers for structuring jobs on a nonstandard basis. Certainly, these workforms offer the possibility of cost savings and flexibility when compared to full-time, more permanent arrangements. The HRPS data offer some evidence that this has been a factor. Survey respondents reported a net increase in the employment of part-time, short-term, and especially independent contract labor; temporary agency personnel represented the only nonstandard workform where more employers reported decreasing rather than increasing use.[18] Establishments were also asked why they em-

18 This is based on unpublished calculations of the HRPS data, which are available from the author.

ployed workers under nonstandard arrangements. The responses suggest that the attraction of these workforms is primarily the flexibility they offer in coping with irregular business levels. While less important than flexibility, controlling labor costs was also a frequently cited reason (Betcherman et al. 1994).[19]

Workplace Training

I have already noted that ILM systems based on low levels of commitment offer little incentive to undertake much training. The basis for this statement is the well-established theoretical and empirical link between enterprise tenure and workplace training. In a recent analysis, for example, the OECD considered this relationship in various ways including jointly comparing job duration and training data across countries and across industries within countries. The clear conclusion was a positive correlation between enterprise tenure and the incidence of workplace training — as the OECD put it, "[t]raining increases with employment stability" (1993, 148).

While Canada was not included in the OECD analysis, one would predict from the relatively high-turnover, low-tenure nature of employment in this country (recall Figure 6) that less workplace training takes place here than in other industrialized countries, where employment relationships are more stable. Indeed, based on data from the late 1980s, I have argued elsewhere (Betcherman 1992) that Canadian firms appear to train less than their counterparts elsewhere, especially those in the lower-left quadrant in Figure 6.

More recent data from the National Training Survey and the Adult Education and Training Survey seem to suggest that the

---

19 While increasing numbers of employers are choosing to structure jobs along nonstandard lines to meet their flexibility or cost objectives, the survey data suggest that many firms will not provide flexible scheduling arrangements in response to requests from employees. Only 28 percent of the HRPS establishments reported that they had arranged jobs to accommodate the preference of employees for nonstandard work.

incidence of workplace training in Canada has increased since that time. However, a close look at the National Training Survey in particular shows that a large proportion of the training activities reported by firms involved training for purposes other than developing the vocational skills of their workers. For example, 26 percent of the training "events" concerned health and safety and another 18 percent was for orientation (Canadian Labour Market and Productivity Centre 1993).

Another significant feature of workplace training in Canada is its tendency to be concentrated among employees who already have relatively high levels of human capital. For example, the Adult Education and Training Survey data indicate that university graduates and workers earning at least $35,000 are more than three times as likely to receive employer-sponsored training than those without postsecondary education or earning less than $20,000.[20]

In an economic environment where there is such a premium placed on responding to change and where technological innovation is pushing up skill requirements, this uneven distribution of workplace training creates adjustment problems for those without access — typically, the lower skilled. Moreover, as I discuss below, it seems likely that this is exacerbating the polarization trend. Finally, the overall low level of investment is a problem given the contribution of human capital to economic growth. While many forms of human resource development can have a positive impact, economic returns are often highest when the process takes place in the work setting.

Earnings Polarization

Increasing earnings inequality and polarization have become an important feature of the labor market in Canada and in a number

---

[20] The sample used for this analysis was restricted to full-time employees with at least one year of enterprise tenure (Kapsalis 1993). To some extent, then, this controls for the possibility that the latter group (that is, those without a postsecondary education) does not have a strong labor force attachment.

of other industrialized countries. Much of what we know about the changing wage distribution is based on data from the United States, where the trend has probably been most marked.

US research has focused on the increasing returns to education — and the attendant widening of education differentials — as an important, if not the most important, polarizing force (Levy and Murnane 1992). This explanation involves both supply and demand factors. On the supply side, the slowdown in the growth of well-educated workers in the 1980s created upward pressure on wages for highly skilled work; at the same time, ongoing trade and investment liberalization effectively increased the (implicit) supply of low-skilled workers, thereby bidding down wages at that end of the distribution. On the demand side, structural and technological change have twisted labor requirements toward highly skilled occupations.

Canadian research has been less extensive and, as a result, testing of the various explanatory hypotheses has been less complete. Some factors that have emerged as important in the United States appear to be significant here as well. For example, Caron (1993) finds evidence that the within-establishment wage dispersion is positively correlated with the extent to which computer-based technology has been introduced. The role of education, however, is not as clear here as it is in the United States: while some analysts have found evidence of increasing returns to education in Canada, others have not.[21]

The most recent, rigorous evidence on earnings distribution trends in Canada highlights the role of two factors in the polarization and increasing inequality: first, a polarization in the overall distribution of hours worked and, second, a widening differential in the relative wages between young workers and the rest of the labor force (Morissette, Myles, and Picot 1993).[22] Another important part of the story (in the United States as well)

---

21 For example, Beach and Slotsve (1993) find increasing returns while Morissette, Myles, and Picot (1993) do not. The reasons for these differing conclusions are discussed in the latter piece.

is that the observed distributional changes are occurring *within* industries. This points to the relevance of firm-level hypotheses and, more specifically, to the role of internal labor markets in explaining the inequality and polarization.

Increasingly, researchers examining distributional trends are speculating on the importance of internal labor markets as explanatory variables (Levy and Murnane 1992; Morissette, Myles, and Picot 1993). To date, though, this has not advanced to a more rigorous stage of analysis. Given what we know about the distributional patterns and about internal labor markets in Canada, however, two groups of potential explanations would seem particularly promising.

The first hinges on differences *between* firms in terms of ILM practices and their distributional implications. In other words, is a wedge being driven between that part of the labor force employed in organizations we have characterized as compensation- and participation-based and those workers in firms with traditional ILM systems? Employees in the former group not only tend to have higher earnings than those in the latter but they also are more likely to have the tenure and training that will raise future earnings. This scenario offers an explanation for the declining relative youth wages, which rests on the difficulties young workers (as "outsiders") have gaining access to employment in the (more desirable) compensation- and participation-based firms. In these firms, long tenure is encouraged (with fewer new hires as a result) and long-tenure employees establish strong property rights to the available jobs.

While this first hypothesis is directed toward between-firm differences, the second focuses on earnings distributions *within*

---

22 US research — for example Burtless (1990) — suggests that the distribution of hourly wages rather than number of hours worked has been more important in that country. Regarding relative wages by age group, Morissette, Myles, and Picot (1993) find that, while prime-age and older workers continued to experience real earnings gains in the 1980s, those under 35 years of age (and especially those under 25) saw their earnings decline significantly.

establishments. It may be that firms that are addressing competitive challenges by focusing on minimizing costs and maximizing flexibility (that is, especially those in the traditional ILM cluster) are moving toward a "core-periphery" type of internal labor market. In this model, employers pursue their strategic objectives by investing heavily in a small core of skilled, well-paid, full-time employees while maintaining a periphery group of less skilled, low-cost nonstandard employees. The polarization of hours, the growth of involuntary nonstandard jobs, and the concentration of workplace training among those who already have considerable amounts of human capital are trends consistent with a core-periphery scenario.

Conclusion

The labor market is changing in ways that are leading to greater economic insecurity for increasing numbers of Canadian workers and their families. The growth in unemployment, in low-wage, nonstandard workforms, and in earnings inequality is creating serious pressures on a social policy framework that was developed for a very different labor market. Clearly, a major challenge for reform will be to modernize programs and institutions to fit well with the new labor market realities.

In this essay, I have considered how changing workplace practices are contributing to the overall employment picture. This focus on employers, or the "demand side," is important in part because so much of the attention of the research and policy communities has been placed on the supply side and the behavior of workers. It is also important because firm strategies around internal labor markets affect the outcomes observed in the external labor market. These linkages must be understood if policymakers are going to respond effectively to the problems of economic insecurity.

While we need to know much more about firm employment practices and their implications for the labor market, there are reasons to be concerned about the level of economic insecurity being generated by these practices. It appears that internal labor markets in most firms — and probably covering most workers — follow a traditional model based on low levels of commitment and involving little investment in the workforce. These employment systems reflect the interest of many employers in maximizing short-run flexibility and cost competitiveness. They also may serve the interests of a core of experienced "insider" employees who are somewhat protected from the risks associated with cyclical, structural, and technological change.

However, these ILM systems generate a large number of short-tenure, nonstandard jobs that offer little economic security either in the short run or the long run. They also have few incentives for investing in human resource development, which constrains the skill formation and the general employability of many workers. Thus, a substantial burden of adjustment is externalized on to the labor market, to those (often young) workers relegated to the insecure job sector, and on to society, which incurs the costs of an increasingly expensive safety net.

In a number of respects, the compensation- and participation-based ILM models reduce the burden placed on the external labor market and on the safety net. If more firms had one of these orientations, we would see more private-sector training, a more employable workforce, and more employment security. Furthermore, a body of evidence is now building which suggests that these high-commitment, high-investment employment systems may also be associated in many situations with better firm performance.[23]

---

23 Although it has not been central to the concerns of this essay, the link to firm performance is obviously an important aspect of the internal labor market question. It is difficult to undertake rigorous analysis, in part because isolating the relationship between workplace practices and performance requires controlling for the host of non-ILM factors that can influence performance. To date, research is most developed in the United States where a body of evidence is building which links high-commitment, high-investment ILM systems with positive performance outcomes. See, for example, the United States (1993). Canadian evidence is reported in Betcherman et al. (1994).

Why, then, are these ILM models not more widely diffused? In the first place, they involve a degree of investment in human resources that simply may not make sense in some industries, especially those with only basic skill needs. And, where that investment does make sense, these models are difficult to adopt. They require a willingness on the part of management and labor to take on roles and responsibilities quite different from those they have been accustomed to.

Moreover, in many respects Canadian institutions and public policies do not support workplace reform along the lines discussed here. For example, the UI system allows employers to externalize the costs of layoffs. Collective bargaining has sustained a tradition of reserved management rights and separable employer and employee interests rather than one of workplace partnerships. Employment standards have created cost advantages associated with the use of nonstandard labor.

Governments cannot legislate a workplace model that encourages flexibility, commitment between the parties, a learning culture, and employee involvement. However, the process of social policy reform would benefit from a careful examination of how current programs and institutions influence the behavior of business and labor in shaping the nature of employment in Canadian workplaces. There are various ways in which the prevailing policy framework might be redirected to reduce the economic insecurity exported by current internal labor market practices.

I have already mentioned the incentives firms have through the UI system to adjust to change through layoffs rather than through internal responses such as retraining and redeployment. This encourages the low-commitment, low-investment ILM approach. Experience-rating UI premiums would direct some of the costs of layoffs to the firms initiating them, thereby creating new incentives to invest in longer-term relationships with their workers.

Certain public benefit and insurance programs also have features which encourage firms toward low-commitment, nonstandard employment forms. A prominent example is the current exemption on UI contributions for employees working less than 15 hours per week. At the same time, through the contribution ceiling, UI creates (as does the Canada Pension Plan) a different type of incentive for firms to direct available work to highly paid employees. Taken together, these regulations support a core-periphery employment strategy and the polarization in the distribution of hours that is behind the growing earnings inequality. This would change by eliminating the ceiling and bringing workers with fewer than 15 weekly hours into the UI system.

Serious consideration should also be given to following Saskatchewan's lead in obliging firms to include part-time workers in employer benefit programs on a prorated basis. The traditional exclusion of part-time and other nonstandard employees was justified on the basis that these tended to be secondary workers without a strong attachment to the employer or to the labor force. The changing nature of nonstandard work has invalidated these assumptions in many cases, with the result that allowing these employees to be excluded from benefit programs has added to their economic insecurity while contributing to the relative cost advantage of nonstandard jobs to employers.

Finally, a case can be made for a greater share of public training funds to be directed toward helping youth make the transition from school to work. Internal labor market practices in most firms offer little opportunity for young workers to move beyond nonstandard status and into the core where training and career development are available. The declining relative youth wages that are an important part of the polarization story reflect the difficulties many young people are experiencing in establishing a foothold in this labor market. School dropouts and others with low levels of educational attainment require more effective "second-chance" programs. In the case of better-educated youth who are still experiencing transition difficulties, selected financial incentives may be needed to induce employers to open up opportunities.

Each of the examples I have discussed concerns a complex matter involving a number of issues. Naturally, the debate over social policy reform must incorporate the full range of considerations, including fiscal factors. In the final analysis, however, workplace practices that increase the investment in human resources and that internalize more of the required adjustment will pay dividends in the labor market and for society more broadly.

References

Beach, C., and G.A. Slotsve. 1993. *Polarization of Earnings in the Canadian Labour Market*. The Bell Canada Papers on Economic and Public Policy. Kingston, Ont.: Queen's University.

Betcherman, G. 1992. "Are Canadian Firms Underinvesting in Training?" *Canadian Business Economics* 1 (Fall).

———, et al. 1994. *The Canadian Workplace in Transition*. Kingston, Ont.: Queen's University IRC Press.

Burtless, G. 1990. "Earnings Inequality Over the Business and Demographic Cycles," in Burtless, ed., *A Future of Lousy Jobs*. Washington, DC: Brookings Institution.

Canadian Labour Market and Productivity Centre. 1993. *National Training Survey*. Ottawa.

Caron, C. 1993. *Technological Change and Internal Labour Markets, 1980-91*. Unpublished background paper. Kingston, Ont.: Queen's University, Industrial Relations Centre.

Doeringer, P.B. and M.J. Piore. 1971. *Internal Labor Markets and Manpower Analysis*. Lexington, Mass.: D.C. Heath.

Economic Council of Canada. 1990. *Good Jobs, Bad Jobs*. Ottawa: Supply and Services Canada.

———. 1991. *Employment in the Service Economy*. Ottawa: Supply and Services Canada.

Hamermesh, D.S. 1994. "Labour Demand: Status and Prospects." In L.N. Christofides et al., eds., *Aspects of Canadian Labor Markets: Essays in Honour of John Vanderkamp*. Toronto: University of Toronto Press.

Kapsalis, C. 1993. "Employee Training in Canada: Reassessing the Evidence." *Canadian Business Economics* 1 (Summer).

Leckie, N. 1994. *Human Resource Management Practices: Patterns and Determinants*. Kingston, Ont.: Queen's University IRC Press.

Levy, F., and R.J. Murnane. 1992. "U.S. Earnings Levels and Earnings Inequality: A Review of Recent Trends and Proposed Explanations." *Journal of Economic Literature* 30 (Summer).

Morissette, R., J. Myles, and G. Picot. 1993. *What Is Happening to Earnings Inequality in Canada?* Research Paper 60. Ottawa: Statistics Canada, Business and Labour Market Analysis Group.

OECD. 1993. *Employment Outlook*. Paris: Organisation for Economic Co-operation and Development.

———. 1994. *The OECD Jobs Study: Facts, Analysis, Strategies*. Paris: Organisation for Economic Co-operation and Development.

Osberg, L. 1994. "The Missing Link: Data on the Demand Side of Labour Markets." Unpublished paper. Department of Economics. Halifax: Dalhousie University.

Osterman, P. 1988. *Employment Futures: Reorganization, Dislocation, and Public Policy*. New York: Oxford University Press.

United States. 1993. Department of Labor. *Report on High Performance Work Practices and Firm Performance*. Washington, DC: Bureau of National Affairs.

Workplace Equity:
A Seat at the Policy Picnic?

Beth Bilson

The notion of equality has had a checkered career in the history of western liberal democracies. The brave eighteenth-century assertion of the civic equality of all citizens was subjected to bracing nineteenth-century allegations that political and economic liberalism, as previously interpreted, had excluded large segments of society from participating in the political process and had been ineffective in bringing about economic security for a wide range of people. This critique of economic and political liberalism became a powerful influence in subsequent policy development in Europe and North America. The formation of government economic and social policies has, for a century or more, been characterized by attempts to achieve a balance that acknowledges the value of individual liberty and the discipline of market forces but at the same time mitigates the harsh effects of extreme *laissez-faire* liberalism on the vulnerable and the disadvantaged.

The dialogue about the policies that will secure the appropriate balance of libertarian and redistributive elements has been based on ideological positions on occasion — though in Canada, at least, less often than one might suppose. Canadian governments have been more pragmatic than dogmatic in their choice of policies since the end of World War II. The Canadian welfare state, which achieved its greatest scope in the 1970s, is a remarkably complicated edifice. Some of its constituents, such as social assistance and income support programs, are clearly meant to have a redistributive effect in favor of people who suffer from social disadvantages. Others, such as publicly funded education (including postsecondary education) and health care, provide benefits to a much wider range of Canadians. Programs such as unemployment insurance and workers' compensation, hardly socialist in their origins, are (in theory, at least) self-financing mechanisms to support the private employment relationship. Public ownership and government operation of utilities are justified on the grounds that the unrestricted operation of market forces tends to monopoly, restricted access, and high prices. Public ownership of natural resources is justified on the grounds that these are part of a national patrimony that should be exploited for the benefit of all citizens, not simply the shareholders of private corporations.

Equality and Equity

The notion of *equality* has long been part of the currency of the policy dialogue. The related concept of *equity* has featured even more prominently in the debate in recent years.

Indeed, the claim that liberal democratic societies are capable of fostering equality has become an important part of the self-definition of western societies, including Canada. A renewed preoccupation with the meaning of equality and with the specific means by which it could be fostered can be seen in the civil rights struggles of blacks and other ethnic minorities in the United States in the 1960s and in the evolution of a new women's movement that can be traced to the same period. These groups expressed frustration with the limited gains possible for them through the assertion of the formal equality guaranteed to them by the liberal state. They argued that a declaration that each person may claim equal participation in society does not sufficiently address the deeply entrenched assumptions, habits, and structures in social institutions that exclude or devalue some members of society. The victims of such processes may enjoy formal equality but they do not have equity.[1]

These groups called for state intervention to confront not only the overt denials of equality that the civil rights campaigns had initially challenged but also the more insidious and intractable kinds of discrimination present in institutions and organizations. This notion of *systemic discrimination*[2] became central to the argument over how true equality could be achieved for all members of society. The idea that much of what retards the achievement of a genuinely equitable society is socially constructed and may be in play even in the absence of consciously discriminatory attitudes has greatly influenced the choice of mechanisms and policy instruments put in place to combat inequality and to allow all members of a society fairer access to its benefits.

---

1 Today, the term "equity" often signals a critical stance with respect to the liberal ideal of equality. Users are often skeptical about the claim that each member of society has an equal value and an equal voice. They invite us to consider whether we make assumptions, establish structures, or follow processes that, without our ever denying that equality is desirable, create barriers to the achievement of genuine equality by many of our compatriots. The connotation of "equity" is that our society is so riddled with such barriers, like the veins in marble, that the assumption that everyone is equal in a democracy is not enough.

   In this paper, I use "equality" primarily to refer to the liberal notion that each citizen has an equivalent stake in society and that each person can, therefore, lay claim to a fixed set of rights and entitlements. I use "equity," on the other hand, to refer to a more dynamic idea: the active consideration of processes or structures and the balancing of interests that are required to achieve a fairer position for the members of Canadian society or of institutions within it. In many contexts, the two words are interchangeable, but I try to change from one to the other in keeping with this distinction.

2 The term is intended to provide a basis for distinguishing between overt or intentional conduct, which is discriminatory, and conduct, organizational structures, and patterns that may be "merely" ingrained, habitual, or thoughtless but nonetheless have a discriminatory impact on individuals or groups. For example, teachers in a school system that values the skills and accomplishments traditionally associated with white male students may ignore or undervalue alternative approaches associated with women or with people from different cultural backgrounds, rendering it difficult for women, aboriginals, and members of visible minorities to gain the same educational status as their white male counterparts.

Entrenching Rights

In the United States, the presence of a bill of rights in the Constitution provided a lever for insistence on renewed attention to equality as a social goal. The roots of that bill were firmly planted in the soil of eighteenth-century liberal and rationalist thought, and the aspirations in the hearts of its framers undoubtedly had more to do with the idea of equality than that of equity. Nonetheless, the constitutional status of equality provided those who espoused new definitions of it with a powerful tool.

The Canadian constitutional structure has no such foundation. A bill of rights passed by Parliament in 1957, often referred to as the "Diefenbaker Bill of Rights," had a somewhat undistinguished existence. In several notable cases,[3] Canadian courts did recognize equality as an important value in the legal system, but the references to the bill of rights in those judgments seem somewhat peripheral and offhanded.

The demand that equality be given high priority as a policy goal was taken quite seriously, however, by Canadian governments of the 1970s. They attempted, in provincial and federal human rights legislation, to devise administrative structures and to articulate criteria through which an attack could be made on all forms of discrimination that might affect Canadians' access to such things as education, employment, and accommodation. The following provision from the Ontario Human Rights Code is typical:

> Sec. 1. Every person has a right to equal treatment with respect to services, goods and facilities without discrimination because of race, ancestry, place of origin, colour, ethnic origin, citizenship, creed, sex, sexual orientation, age, marital status, family status or handicap.

---

3 For example, *Roncarelli v. Duplessis* (1959), 16 DLR (2d) 689 (SCC).

This kind of legislation made it possible for individuals who complained of discrimination to have their allegations investigated and adjudicated by human rights commissions clothed with certain remedial powers.

In addition to this power to address individual complaints, the legislation also gave human rights commissions an important educational role and the capacity to consider remedies for discrimination in a broad sense. Perhaps the most noteworthy of these remedies was what has been variously labeled "reverse discrimination" or "affirmative action":[4] programs by which attempts would be made to produce a pattern in an institution that would redress historical underrepresentation of particular groups. This remedy, more than any other factor, has led to a debate that has an increasingly intemperate note.

The Charter

The human rights legislation of the 1970s was formulated at a provincial level and did not enshrine aversion to discrimination as a national value. The constitutionalization of equality took place in the early 1980s, as part of a package of constitutional reforms on a variety of issues that had featured as perennial topics of Canadian political discussion — the relationship of Canada with Great Britain, multiculturalism, and the status of francophone Canadians among them.

The entrenchment of a Charter of Rights and Freedoms, which was proposed by the federal government, was not greeted with universal acclaim. The premier of Saskatchewan, Allan Blakeney, was one of the most vocal critics of entrenchment, then and later, primarily on the grounds that a constitutional bill of rights would shift the locus of decisionmaking on these important

---

4 In the 1984 report of the Ontario Royal Commission on Equity in Employment, Madam Justice Rosalie Abella suggested the use of terms such as "employment equity," given the negative associations surrounding the terms quoted here.

issues from elected politicians to nonelected judges. In spite of such objections, the Charter did emerge as part of the deal struck in 1981.

Section 15 of the Charter of Rights and Freedoms, enacted in the *Constitution Act, 1982*, accords each Canadian the right to equality in the following terms:

> 15(1) Every individual is equal before and under the law and has the right to the equal protection and equal benefit of the law without discrimination based on race, national or ethnic origin, colour, religion, sex, age or mental or physical disability.

Other provisions of the Charter prohibit discrimination on many of the grounds mentioned in provincial human rights codes.

The enshrinement of the concept of equality in the Constitution gave a new basis to the claims of those individuals and groups who argue that they do not enjoy equal status in Canadian society. The provisions of the Charter enjoy pre-eminent legal status, and this starting point has allowed an examination of institutional structures, legislation, and conduct according to the criterion of equality to an extent that was not possible before. From the question of whether girls should be allowed to play on hockey teams to that of whether Canadian citizenship is a legitimate requirement for membership in a provincial law society to whether women have been unfairly excluded from employment on railways,[5] the measuring stick of equality is being applied to the position and entitlements of Canadians at work, at home, at school, and in all the activities of their daily lives.

Judicial discussion of the significance of section 15 of the Charter quickly made it clear that the courts saw this provision as requiring a distinction between *formal equality* and *substantive equality*. By the former phrase, the judges alluded to the

---

5 Respectively, *Blainey v. Ontario Hockey Association* (1986), 26 DLR (4th) 728; (leave to appeal to SCC refused [1986] 1 SCR xii); *Andrews v. Law Society of British Columbia* (1989), 56 DLR (4th) 1; [1989] 1 SCR 143; *Action Travail des Femmes v. CNR* (1987), 40 DLR (4th) 193; [1987] 1 SCR 1114.

liberal notion that all citizens should be treated alike and recognized as enjoying an equal position in Canadian society. Though this concept might be important in some contexts, the courts saw an exclusive focus on it as permitting the construction and perpetuation of inequalities of a substantive nature because the idea of formal equality cannot take completely into account the distinctions and positions of relative power that exist in society.

Beyond the Charter

The Charter itself purports, under section 32, to regulate only the activities and enactments of governments and their emanations. The question, then, is whether the section 15 guarantee of equality has any relevance to relations between private parties, including all aspects of the relationship between employees and private sector employers. Two things should be noted here. First, even without a guarantee of equality enjoying the force of a constitutional provision, the notion of equality and the jurisprudence that has emerged under section 15 have been important constituents of the interpretation of other legislation that enjoins discrimination. Second, the existence and importance of section 15 has served as a focal point for the growth in self-consciousness and the articulation of the aspirations of groups that claim that their fortunes have been negatively affected by discrimination.

Since 1982, the assault on discrimination has thus been carried on both by courts faced with challenges based on the Charter and by human rights commissions operating under provincial legislation. Completing the picture are developments at the provincial level that, in some sense, represent refinements or augmentations of existing structures under human rights legislation. Ontario, for example, has established specialist tribunals to deal with issues of pay equity (inequalities in wages) and employment equity (inequities in hiring and advancement). (Other issues defined in the Human Rights Code still lie under the mandate of the Human Rights Commission.) In Saskatchewan, recent amendment to the *Occupational Health and Safety Act* treats harassment, including sexual and racial harassment, in the workplace as a health and safety issue. (It had previously been defined and dealt with exclusively by the Human Rights Commission.)

The Mood of the 1990s

The activities of courts and administrative bodies such as human rights tribunals have doubtless had considerable influence on Canadian institutions and organizations in the past decade, and issues of equity have been very prominent in public and political discussion during this period. At the same time, however, the critique of the existing mechanisms and the principles they espouse has been vigorous. Perhaps it is easier to be gracious about the idea of equality in good times than in bad. The commentary on issues of equity shows increasing signs of weariness, bitterness, and sourness, laced with professions of anxiety about the size of the public debt. Legislative programs are attacked for being cumbersome, expensive, unfair, and ridiculous, for interfering with the operation of market forces, for catering to special interest groups, for kowtowing to the forces of "political correctness." In particular, there are calls for the diminution of state intervention in private matters such as employment, and charges that the distribution of jobs and promotions on the basis of any criteria other than merit and productivity is unfair and damaging to the effective operation of the economy.

Public institutions and policies, such as those I have described, are, of course, fair game for vigorous scrutiny and debate. They must be open to continuing reappraisal, revision — and elimination if that is advisable. Whether particular legislation is sufficiently clear and precise to govern the work of an administrative tribunal, whether that tribunal may have misconceived its mandate, whether a tribunal functioning under a statute is a more or less appropriate instrument than a court in relation to a particular issue — all these questions are legitimate subjects for public debate and legislative deliberation. I argue, however, that the legal mechanisms currently in place do have an important role to play in upholding the value of equality in Canadian society and in achieving advances toward equity in the workplace.

Notice that I am proceeding on the assumption that the notion of equality is a legitimate objective for public policies concerning employment. This statement seems a bland enough profession of faith. Nonetheless, the current discussion of "political correctness," much of which is vehement in tone, has forced advocates of equality in social, political, and economic institutions to restate their loyalties in fundamental terms. In my view, the protections for equality that exist under provincial and federal human rights legislation, in the Charter of Rights and Freedoms, and in the interpretations administrative tribunals and the courts give these enactments have come about through the legitimate activity of the legitimate institutions of a democratic society. Though critics sometimes describe these changes as though they had been engineered by relatively small groups of especially committed people, they were in fact the product of extensive public and legislative discussion.[6]

The particular terms in which the protections accorded to equality are expressed and their application to particular factual circumstances should continue to be subject to public scrutiny and open debate. It should be remembered, however, that they have come into existence because of conscious decisions by governments whose authority stems from their valid election as representatives of the population and by tribunals and judges who have not exceeded the jurisdiction or mandate accorded to them under current constitutional and legislative arrangements.

The dismissive and pejorative use of terms such as "interest group politics" to describe the process of formulating policies and

---

6 In the case of the Charter in particular, it seems possible that public disaffection with politicians and legislatures moved many to place an unusual degree of faith in the courts.

devising mechanisms to support the goal of equity further seems to characterize the issue as one exclusively related to the interests of minority groups and those on the margins of Canadian society. The corollary is that it is somehow unfair to push equity issues to a prominent place on the policy agenda when the majority of Canadian citizens do not stand to benefit and, furthermore, have troubles of their own.

This line of thinking seems to me to ignore the fact that a commitment to equality lies at the core of Canadian ideas of democracy and civic virtue. The pressure groups currently held responsible for skewing the development of public policy are attacking not the idea of equality but the ineffectiveness of liberal assumptions in producing genuine equality across a citizenry diverse in its character. Moreover, it is not the success of pressure group politics that has brought about experimentation with new mechanisms aimed at equity. Indeed, groups such as women, the disabled, and aboriginal people in Canada have not been particularly militant, well organized, or influential. Steps have been taken toward achievement of their goals because those goals appeal to ordinary citizens and politicians whose politics are grounded in perfectly orthodox notions of fairness and equality.

The Purpose of This Paper

I believe one can have a fruitful discussion of the place that considerations of equity can or should have in policies related to the workplace without taking an extreme or definitive position on individual issues, such as pay equity or mandatory retirement, or even on more general issues, such as the exclusivity that the market should enjoy in determining all issues related to employment. I am not making any attempt to establish a comprehensive program for the achievement of equity in the Canadian workplace. I seek only to draw attention to some factors that may give clues to why and how to incorporate this concept into discussions of appropriate policies.

Finally, I warn that this paper is concerned only with policies related to the terms and conditions of employment and other structures in the workplace itself, not with policies related to job creation or the stimulation of regional employment. Though an analysis of such policies might show some of the comments made here to be relevant, this essay does not direct itself to that area of policymaking.

The examples I use here are drawn from the workplace, though many of the points they illustrate could clearly be made about other situations, such as education. I begin by suggesting that neither the market nor other existing structures, of which the most important is collective bargaining, have been completely effective in protecting equality for Canadian workers. I then suggest some of the strengths and shortcomings of legal mechanisms, such as the interpretation of the Charter, and of provincial human rights legislation. Next, after sketching some history, I consider some inherent challenges for policymakers: the dual meanings in many kinds of equality; the interaction of different kinds of equality; and holistic reality in which collective and individual rights are inseparable and the marketplace cannot be divided from the family and other social institutions.

The Market

I suggested earlier that Canadian policy has not subscribed to an unmodified liberal theory of the market over the past century. Though such theory has become more prominent in the political rhetoric of the past 15 years, the market red in tooth and claw has not been a determinative feature of political and economic life in this country. Canadian policymakers have acknowledged that market forces alone cannot be trusted to secure all citizens just desserts for an investment of their labor.

Analysis of wage structures, for example, reveals the existence of a stubborn wage differential that can be explained only by discrimination on the basis of gender (Treiman and Hartmann

1981; Robb 1987).[7] "Normal" factors, such as differences in training and women's absence from the labor market to pursue family responsibilities cannot explain this male-female wage gap. Discrimination on the basis of race also seems to create a wage gap (Treiman and Hartmann 1981).[8]

The existence of such a divergence should not be surprising. One of the features of market-driven structures is the room they create for the exercise of personal preferences. If discriminatory attitudes are present in society — a proposition that hardly seems debatable — then it stands to reason that such attitudes are reflected in the market choices: the employees who are hired, the jobs they are assigned, the wages they are paid, and so on.

Market Explanations of the Gender Gap

What is the nature of the gender gap in earnings? Mainstream economists accept that the difference exists. They explain it in part by reference to the workings of the market, which have made female workers available at lower wages and have produced crowding — and, therefore, downward pressure on wages — in those parts of the labor market most frequented by women. Paula England (1992) suggests that this characterization applies the operation of preference in the market to one aspect but not to another important contributor to gender-differentiated wage patterns:

> I believe that there is an inconsistency in the neoclassical
> view that crowding is the sole source of discriminatory wages
> in women's jobs. In this view, employers devalue female *labor*
> for certain jobs such that they will not hire women unless they
> work for a lower wage than would be offered men. The

---

7 There have been recent signs that the gap is slowly closing. Analysts speculate, however, that this change owes more to declines in wages for men than to improvements in the wages of women. See Sorensen (1991, 128–129); "Male Female Wage Gap," *Saskatoon Star-Phoenix*, January 17, 1994.

8 There is, however, a dearth of work in Canada exploring the scope and nature of race as a ground of wage discrimination. Analysis of the wage effects of physical or mental disability is also in its infancy.

devaluation of female labour is generally seen as motivated by tastes, statistical generalization, or group collusion. Yet, in seeing this as the sole discriminatory source of low wages in women's jobs, neoclassical writers implicitly reject the possibility that employers devalue certain jobs or job characteristics because of their present or historic association with women. But surely if the first devaluation is plausible, the second is as well. If employers tend to underestimate the value of women's labor for a given job in the hiring process, surely it is likely that they also tend to underestimate the contribution of the work done in women's jobs to the organization's productivity. Much of the radical/cultural/feminist view...centers on the fact that spheres of human endeavor associated with women have been systematically deprecated in Western thought and institutions. (Ibid., 117.)

In other words, the role the market accords choices and preferences may disguise and support the exercise of discriminatory attitudes in the workplace. Since the choices that establish market value are made by human beings who are immersed in the social base from which they operate, those choices are inevitably colored by a social discourse in which particular notions of what constitutes "efficiency" or "good public relations" or even a "neat appearance" prevail.

It is true, of course, that some employers cash in on these socially determined attitudes by picking up undervalued female labor at bargain rates. (Such behavior does not work toward ameliorating the wage gap, though it may address unemployment.) For other employers, however, adherence to their unexamined assumptions is simply part of the cost of doing business.

The Failure of Market Explanations

Although some versions of market theory do not claim to provide a comprehensive explanation for the behavior of actors in the labor market, many fail to take sufficient account of a number of factors that are significant from the point of view of public policy.

For example, the intractability of a discriminatory wage pattern reflects the relative power of employers and their preferences in the workplace. Neoclassical purists may characterize workers and employers as having equivalent positions in the labor market, but public policy has long recognized that workers as individuals do not enjoy a power to contract that is truly equal to that of their employers. North American collective bargaining legislation was founded on this premise 50 years ago, and other statutory schemes, such as labor standards and occupational health and safety legislation, similarly acknowledge that workers cannot exercise absolute control over the terms on which they will supply their labor or the conditions in which they will consent to work.

Neither can market explanations be accepted as the sole sources of information in which policy is grounded. The assumptions on which such explanations rest are not neutral with respect to such matters as race and gender. They do not place sufficient emphasis on the interconnections between the labor market and other social, political, legal, and cultural aspects of individual and community life.

Consider, for example, the nature of the experience, training, and responsibility of workers before they enter the labor market, while they may be absent from it, and after they leave it. It is clear that members of groups in Canadian society defined by gender, race, or disability do not have equal access to educational and training opportunities, and that they may not have equal capacity to benefit from the ones they do have. In some cases, they may also be disadvantaged in terms of social skills, nutrition, health and fitness, coordination, or other characteristics that have some relevance to their employment selection or assessment. The extent to which employers and other actors in the labor market should be held responsible for redressing discrimination that occurs outside the sphere of market activity in which they operate is, of course, another question. The implications of pervasive discrimination are, however, clearly a relevant consideration in terms of the formulation of public policy.

The effect of market choices once workers have entered the labor market is also a significant question. Personal choices and objectively defined qualifications play a prominent role in the movement of workers to particular industries or occupational groups, and these choices may be, in part, responsible for variations in wages. The definitions of specific job classifications, however, are to some extent contaminated by social constructions of gender or race. McDermott (1991a, 28) gives a striking example: the value allotted to the skill involved in using a screwdriver but not a syringe and the calculation of extra recompense for "men's dirt" such as axle grease, but not for the vomit and urine encountered by health care workers. Another example is the presumption of physical weakness on the part of women or older workers. Yet another is the characterization of certain cultural characteristics — diffidence or formality, for instance — as unsuitable in jobs that entail contact with the public (though that public may include people who would find those characteristics familiar).

Clearly, the setting of wage rates for particular jobs is a complicated matter and one in which there are no tablets of stone to provide absolute standards. I suggest, however, that a willingness to acknowledge pervasive social assumptions about different kinds of work and to take them into account as part of the process of considering appropriate wage levels would be an important step toward achieving equity. This would be the case whether wage levels were being set unilaterally by employers, through collective bargaining with trade unions, or within a framework of legislative enactments and adjudicative decisionmaking.

The Role of Bureaucracy

In the increasingly bureaucratic organization of the modern workplace, I believe that the exercise of preferences in the selection and advancement of employees has become insulated from the direct discipline of market forces to a significant extent. Though, in general terms, the market may "punish" an enterprise for making choices that do not rest on "real" considerations related to efficiency and productivity, the bureaucratic structure of many organizations surely creates a great deal of room for making decisions in which assumptions related to race, gender, or physical ability have an influence.

The definition of the expected qualifications and responsibilities of an employee occupying a particular position rests largely, after all, with the management of an enterprise, and much of the process of definition and assessment rests on subjective judgments of various kinds and on somewhat arbitrary standards. It is hard to accept, for example, that the inevitable operation of market forces requires particular discriminatory definitions or expectations of an "Accounts Receivable Clerk II" or a "Vice-President (Customer Services)" or an "Oxygen Therapy Technician Assistant." It is not so much the market as social conditioning that provides much of the input into the descriptions of such classifications. In themselves, they are largely blank pages on which one can write "men have good heads for figures," or "women are generally content to be in subordinate, clerical positions," "people from visible minorities are likely to lack the language skills to deal with customers appropriately," or "men are more extroverted and more likely to have a commitment to the company," "men are better at technical things," or "women are less likely to challenge the authority of the doctors in charge."

Do those responsible for selecting and assessing employees allow their male executives to spend afternoons playing golf (license in the name of public relations) while making notional black marks against the names of female executives who spend afternoons with sick children (censure in the name of lack of commitment)? Do they exclude certain groups of employees, such as part-time workers, from information about opportunities for advancement, assuming they would be unsuitable or not interested? Do they fail to seriously consider minor accommodations that might make it possible for employees with physical disabilities to occupy certain positions?

In my view, it is unrealistic to suppose that the operation of market forces can be focused to test these and similar questions. The concepts of merit and necessary qualifications are too slippery and the links between modern management structures and market forces too indirect to prevent socially entrenched constructions of race and gender from continuing to have a discriminatory effect in employment. Yet any consideration of how to produce an equitable workplace requires recognizing that the placement of employees in certain jobs and the calibration of their wages are susceptible to being affected by our views about race, gender, and disability.

Globalization and International Competition

The Canadian workplace, like the economy as a whole, has changed much over the past decade or so. The expectations of those who battled for the passage of human rights legislation and for the inclusion in the Charter of protections against discrimination seem, in retrospect, to have been based on the assumption that a strong economy operating through familiar institutions would smooth the way for rapid advancement toward the goal of equality. They may have been overoptimistic.

The growing emphasis on economic restructuring in the face of new global pressures has presented new challenges to advocates of equity.[9] Canadian employers' adoption of strategies such as introducing new technologies, downsizing the work force, enhancing flexibility by the increased use of part-time workers, moving into the services sector, and referring to global cost comparisons as a means of exerting pressure on wage costs has pushed the issue of equity to the sidelines to a significant extent, as workers scramble to protect their employment. At the same time, a new and vigorous critique of the scope and role of the

9 For a full discussion of the implications of many of these changes for economic policy, see Courchene (1987; 1994).

public sector in the economy has raised new questions about the desirability of using government as an instrument for the advancement of equality.

Advocates of pay and employment equity and other policies intended to counteract discrimination express concern about the implications of these trends in the economy. Bakker (1991, 271) argues, for example, that the steps adopted by Canadian employers to meet the challenges of international competition and globalization have a disproportionate impact on groups of workers, such as women, who are concentrated in jobs characterized by low skills and low pay.

As Bakker (ibid.) points out , it is not yet clear what impact these current economic trends will have on particular categories of workers. What is a matter for concern is the extent to which preoccupation with the economic consequences of globalization and international competition has dampened or silenced discussion of the legitimate aspirations of Canadian workers who have not been treated equitably. By talking of market forces on a global scale as given, those responsible for the direction of the Canadian economy in recent years have increasingly shifted the debate about how to meet the challenges of globalization so as to fit a paradigm based on the premise of a deregulated, international marketplace.

The principle that policy issues should not fetter the free operation of market forces is clearly relevant to many things besides the goal of equality for Canadian workers as they live their working lives and prepare for their withdrawal from the workforce. Since the conclusion of successive free trade agreements, for example, challenges to Canadian public policies have increasingly put before the public the question of what should be regarded as the distinctive and irreducible features of a Canadian economic and social system. There has been growing discussion of the degree to which participation in the international marketplace requires reversing public policy choices made in the past, some more prized than others, that are manifest in social programs, in the tax system, and in legislation concerning labor and employment.

The question of whether and how the objective of equitable terms and conditions of employment for working Canadians should be pursued is thus one of a range of issues that have for some time been regarded as peripheral to the "real" issues facing the Canadian economy. At this point, relatively little analysis has been done to suggest the probable results of the interplay of global and domestic factors (including both market forces and policy choices) or to predict the different results that might occur if different weights were given to particular factors. The question of the price Canadians are willing to pay — in financial terms or in more intangible considerations, such as working conditions — is, however, being raised more frequently and in an increasingly pointed way, as items such as health care, unemployment insurance, sales taxes, cultural subsidies, and labor standards are held up for scrutiny against the provisions and underlying assumptions of international conventions and agreements. As Canadians embark on a new kind of debate about these issues, it is surely appropriate to ask that the formulation of public policy create a space for consideration of the widest possible range of factors so that the true costs, economic and otherwise, of various options may be fully considered.

My purpose in raising these points is not to suggest that the market has no proper role in influencing levels of wages and other aspects of working life. Rather, in arguing for explicit provision for considerations of equality, I am suggesting that to concentrate too heavily on the operation of market forces is to focus the making of public policy too narrowly. Policymaking must take into consideration not only levels of wages and other conditions in the workplace but also the interplay between work as an economic commodity and work as a socially valued activity, the value to be accorded to the production of family and home life and recreation, the expectations we are prepared to allow our elders to nurture, and the purposes and nature of educational and cultural development. The connections between the workplace and other institutions in society must be a serious subject for the policymaker. Policymaking that adhered dogmatically to market-based ideas without reference to the family and other social institutions, to historical antecedents, to legitimate social and political goals would be policy formation in a vacuum indeed.

Collective Bargaining

The institution of collective bargaining has been one of the major influences modifying the free operation of market forces in the workplace. There is much controversy over the extent to which it directly affects wage levels, but there is no doubt that collective agreements give employers obligations, particularly with respect to employee advancement and termination, that prevent them from responding in all circumstances to what they perceive to be the demands of the market. Proponents of collective bargaining argue that it does not remove enterprises from the reach of market forces but simply ensures that the response to the market is devised in a way that takes into account the interests of the workers.

No one seems to have suggested that the attainment of equality for all workers can safely be left entirely to the workings of the institution of collective bargaining, the traditional means by which groups of workers have sought to achieve greater influence and better conditions in their employment. Indeed, in setting up statutory mechanisms aimed at achieving equity, policymakers have given little attention to how they might be most compatible with the configuration of negotiations, agreements, and procedures for the resolution of disputes that characterize collective bargaining relationships.

The Divisive Potential

Equity is, in some respects, an issue that trade unions are well suited to consider. They are democratic institutions whose primary loyalty is not to an enterprise's bottom line but to their members' interests, very broadly defined. As Aldrich and Buchele (1986, 42) point out, an issue such as pay equity might be expected to provide a rallying cry for the organizing of groups of workers who have traditionally resisted unionization and who might have much to gain from policies concentrating on equity.

Equity has also proved, however, to have a divisive potential for trade unions, and advocates of equity programs have, in turn, been reluctant to entrust unions with exclusive responsibility for the pursuit of equality for workers. One reason is, of course, that trade unions, like other social institutions, have not themselves been perfectly free of discriminatory practices and assumptions. The white male workers who have had the predominant influence in union leadership and the formulation of collective bargaining positions in large part share their employers' assumptions about the appropriate ranking of jobs, the needs of male and female workers, and the status of part-time workers.

Trade unions have also been suspicious that gains for those of their members who suffer from disadvantage may have to be paid for at the bargaining table by those workers on whose behalf they have had some success. For example, trade unions have been wary about becoming involved in the sort of job evaluation exercise that is the basis of many of the current policies directed at pay equity. Indeed, McDermott (1991b, 131) suggests that unions' input into the definition of job classifications has been largely through the grievance procedure.

Unions' experience with bargaining lends some credence to their concern about the implications of pay and employment equity. Wages and salaries are a costly item for employers, and they naturally resist changes that will increase these costs. Collective bargaining cannot be viewed as an entirely open-ended, elastic process.[10]

---

10 Even in the case of challenges to mandatory retirement — a topic we shall revisit — trade unions have in general defended the existing arrangements, fearing that the abandonment of a uniform retirement age would jeopardize pension plans and the advancement of other workers.

Thus, some people see trade unions and the collective bargaining system not as a constructive vehicle for forwarding the objective of equity but as barriers to the achievement of this goal. As trade unions claim to represent the weak in the face of the powerful, there are those who would claim to speak for the relatively weak *within* trade unions in the face of complacent or biased leaders. McDermott (1991b, 131–132) suggests, for example, that a prudent strategy for advocates of pay equity is to have these issues decided independently of collective bargaining.

A Useful Instrument of Change

In some respects, the charge that collective bargaining has not been an adequate means of advancing workplace equity is well founded. There is some basis for an argument that collective bargaining has been an instrument for the "haves" among the workforce, as much a way of maintaining the status quo for privileged workers as for advancing the cause of more disadvantaged workers, among whom are disproportionate numbers of women, aboriginal people, members of visible minorities, and the disabled. It must also be acknowledged that there will continue to be difficulties in fitting the objective of equity into the current collective bargaining system, in arriving at collective agreements that reflect that objective without unseemly compromises, and in assuring that collective bargaining does not become the repository of expectations that it will always disappoint.

On the other hand, the trade unions that represent workers and the bargaining process in which they engage on behalf of those workers can be useful instruments in bringing the objective of equity to the workplace in a manner that matches the aspirations of particular groups of workers in specific settings. Although far from perfect, trade unions are democratic organizations, responsive to their members and accountable to them constitutionally and through the legal duty of fair representation. Collective bargaining represents one means of bringing the discussion of equity standards into the particular context to which they are expected to apply. It is a process in which the interests of both employer and workers must be considered and through which the parties may devise mechanisms or procedures that serve their mutual needs.

Many trade unions — particularly those, such as the Canadian Union of Public Employees, that have large numbers of women members — have accepted the challenge and embraced equity as an issue that must be given increasing attention. The Canadian Labour Congress (1993) recently issued a policy document stating its support for affirmative action programs, acknowledging that this stance might have an impact on collective agreement provisions based on seniority. The United Steelworkers of America has concluded a number of agreements in the mining industry that include preferential terms for aboriginal workers.

I believe that collective bargaining, in spite of its shortcomings, provides a means whereby all issues affecting the terms and conditions under which employees work, including issues of equity, can be subjected to rigorous scrutiny and discussion within the framework provided by the realities the parties face. There are of course, other models. The costs of achieving equity might be shifted entirely to the shoulders of the taxpayer, for example, or imposed as an additional obligation on employers through the independent determination suggested by McDermott (1991b, 131–132). Collective bargaining does, however, provide a useful vehicle for the pursuit of equity. Neither its agenda nor its outcome is fixed.

Under these conditions, it is open to trade unions and employers to make an honest examination of their own workplace with considerations of equity in mind and to set realistic standards for achieving it. Although it is unlikely that equality in the workplace, or anywhere else, can be achieved entirely by leaving it to the participants to decide how to move in that direction (Abella 1987), the possibilities offered by collective bargaining, which provides a ready-made forum for the sorting of interests, the consideration of options, and the mediation of positions, should not be underrated as a means of moving toward equity.

Legal Mechanisms

I suggested earlier that the law has played its role in relation to the issue of equality on two different stages: one set in the courts against a backdrop of the Charter, and the other framed by legislative provisions and administrative programs. The latter include statutory attempts to confront the issues of equity directly, such as human rights codes, and legislation dealing with pay and employment equity.[11]

The Charter and the Courts

The work of the courts, particularly the Supreme Court of Canada, in interpreting the Charter has been the subject of considerable discussion since 1982. Whether or not Pierre Trudeau and its other anxious parents foresaw the implications of constitutional entrenchment of the rights it describes, the changes this development has wrought in Canadian legal tradition can hardly be overstated. Formerly, the doctrine of parliamentary supremacy meant that common law courts gave legislative provisions priority in making decisions. The Charter has had the effect of according to certain rights, stated in a very absolute and comprehensive form, the status of constitutional trump cards that Ca-

---

11 They also include statutory provisions aimed at the protection of disadvantaged workers that do not explicitly address the concept of equity. For example, recently enacted amendments to the Saskatchewan *Labour Standards Act* require that employment benefits available to full-time employees be prorated for part-time employees. Since a large proportion of part-time employees are women, this provision may be expected to have some effect on historic disadvantages suffered by women workers.

nadian citizens can play against the state in the absence of compelling justification. Thus, the provisions of the Charter have proved an open invitation to judicial activism of a kind with which Canadians were not very familiar (though the US experience provided an instructive example).

One can argue that the entrenchment of rights in the Charter and the provision for vindication of those rights through the judicial process are essential as a statement of vital Canadian values. The enshrining of these rights, which have the ring of natural law about them, and the availability of the highest judicial bodies as the means of achieving enforcement are no doubt a potent national symbol. Indeed, many of the decisions made by courts, particularly the Supreme Court of Canada and the provincial appeal courts, have been complex and thoughtful pieces of work, revealing that Canadian judges have a capacity for analysis of public values that they previously did not have to call on often. The courts are in a unique position to present such issues for intellectual consideration.[12]

The decade or so since proclamation of the Charter has also, however, revealed some of the shortcomings of constitutional interpretation by the courts as a means of advancing equality. The occasions for interpretation of the Charter are not selected entirely on the basis of their general significance or their universality of application.[13] Rather, they are presented as the assertion of an individual's rights in a specific context.

The case of Merv Lavigne[14] illustrates both the advantages and the shortcomings of the judicial process as a means of articulating important political values. Mr. Lavigne, who was on the faculty of a community college, was not a member and was

---

12 Though it must be admitted that there has been relatively little exploitation of this opportunity by the press or the public, bemused perhaps by the rarefied discussions emanating from Canadian law schools.

13 Though the Supreme Court of Canada can refuse to hear a case on the grounds that it is not of sufficient national import.

14 *Lavigne v. OPSEU* (1993), 81 DLR (4th) 545 (SCC).

not required to be a member of the union that represented him
and his colleagues. Under the union security provisions of the
collective agreement, he was, however, required to pay dues to
the union. He raised an objection to paying at least part of these
dues on the grounds that they were used in support of the New
Democratic Party, the Ontario Federation of Labour, and causes,
such as opposition to the building of the Toronto Skydome, with
which he did not agree. He argued that forcing his indirect
financial participation in these activities, which were not connected directly with the determination of his terms and conditions of employment, violated the freedom of association
guaranteed him by the Charter.

The decision of the Supreme Court of Canada was complex,
but the gist of the majority decision was that the important public
purpose served by trade unions justified the modest invasion of
Mr. Lavigne's right to control the destination of his money and
thus his freedom of association. This decision was a striking
assertion by the Supreme Court of the view that the exercise of
individual rights must on occasion give way to collective or public
interests. One can hardly overstate the authority of such a
pronouncement from the senior court of the nation. On the other
hand, the court's decision was shaped by the peculiarities of the
context in which the case arose. Since Mr. Lavigne was not
required to be a member of the union, the question of compulsory
union membership as such was not directly before the court
(though much of the discussion had implications for that issue).
Some of the other rare occasions on which the Supreme Court has
addressed the significance of collective bargaining concerned the
constitutionality of provincial wage-control legislation,[15] an important scenario but hardly a typical one.

The form of all of these actions is an individual's assertion
of rights and demand for redress. Though public officials repre-

---

15 See, for example, *Public Service Alliance v. The Queen in Right of Canada*
   (1987) 87 CLLC 14, 022 (SCC); *Retail, Wholesale and Department Store Union
   v. Government of Saskatchewan* (1987) 87 CLLC 14, 023 (SCC)

senting provincial governments speak in cases in which constitutional issues are raised and other bodies may intervene in the name of some more general interest, using this opportunity to raise issues of public policy, the case is always fundamentally focused on an individual or limited group and a particular set of circumstances. The possibility of comparing a wide range of similar cases is limited, since only a small number of cases of the same type reach the courts, especially the Supreme Court.

Another source of frustration for those who were optimistic about the potential of the Charter as a vehicle for claiming equality is the cumbersome and costly nature of the judicial process. This concern is not, of course, limited to cases involving constitutional interpretation, but it seems particularly ironic that claims for equality under the Charter are inhibited by the very economic and social disadvantages that are the basis of those claims. Though bodies such as the Court Challenges Program, which is government supported, and the Legal Education and Action Fund (LEAF), which is a charitable organization, have taken some steps to provide funding or intervention in cases selected for their public importance, it is certainly not possible for all potential claimants to pursue an action in the courts.

Tribunals and Administrative Agencies

Judicial decisionmaking's focus on the assertion of rights by individuals helps to define the scope of the results that emerge from it. Though judicial decisions do contain statements of principle that have application to society as a whole, the remedies the courts order are aimed at redressing wrongs to individuals rather than reordering a social structure. In other words, the regime is remedial with limited educational or transformative capacity, aside from the potency of individual example.

In this respect, adjudicative tribunals and administrative bodies operating under statutory provisions have something of an advantage. Bodies such as human rights commissions do have an adjudicative mandate, which means that they consider complaints based on individuals' or groups' assertion of rights in something of the same way that courts do. On the other hand, such specialized tribunals consider a great many cases arising from similar circumstances and thus are able to develop a stronger sense of context and of comparison of one case to another. Furthermore, those bodies have a mandate that comprehends other means of advancing the legislative objects underlying the statutes. Their responsibilities include enhancing public education and assisting in social change. A human rights commission, for example, not only provides for the adjudication of particular complaints but may also assist organizations and enterprises in articulating equity-related goals for themselves and in devising plans for achieving those goals.

Like all human organizations, the tribunals and agencies charged with advancing the goal of bringing about equity in Canadian workplaces may function well or badly. That their objectives may be ill defined, their governing legislation badly drafted, their resources insufficient, or their staff incompetent does not, however, lead me to conclude that they should be abolished. Rather, I believe that these bodies play a necessary role in supporting the legitimate public goal of securing more equitable circumstances for Canadian workers. The articulation of objectives, the gathering and dissemination of information, the comparison of one set of circumstances with another, the facilitation of self-appraisal, and the opportunity for detached evaluation — all these, I argue, are dimensions of the development of policy in this area that cannot be left completely to the operation of market forces or other mechanisms that concentrate on individual enterprises. There must, I think, be a social lens brought to bear on these issues. In this scheme, the adjudication of rights-based complaints plays an important symbolic and retributive role, but that is not the exclusive — or even perhaps the most important — function of administrative tribunals and agencies.

The Sweep of History

The considerable changes in the nature and approach of many rights-oriented agencies and tribunals, as well as the introduction of new legislation and new administrative structures, bespeak the fact that administrative policy in this area is still in a highly malleable and formative state. Policymakers at both the administrative and political level still have a long row to hoe to achieve a balanced and effective way of achieving their goals with respect to equity.

Before we go on to several of the challenges inherent in attempts to devise policies of this kind, I want to insert an advertisement for history. It is difficult to make sensible policy decisions without examining the historical antecedents of the system that is currently in place. The base on which this structure is laid consists, at least in part, of the remains of past events, judgments, and values.

Current wage patterns, for example, cannot be understood merely by examining them on their own terms. Rather, they derive from cultural and social practices and values that have become deeply engrained and that must be reviewed in order to divine the significance of the structures they have produced.[16] One of the challenges for administrative agencies engaged in implementing policy objectives related to equity is to reach some coherent conclusion about history's implications for current policy.

A Living Wage...A Family Wage

In her analysis of the historical evolution of the concept of pay equity, Kessler-Harris (1992) demonstrates that the historical origins of wage structures influence the understanding we have

---

16 A historical examination of other aspects of the terms and conditions of employment — mandatory retirement, for example, or parental leave, political leave, advancement opportunities, or degree of supervision — would reveal similarly stubborn roots of custom and practice.

of them. Revealing the deep historical roots of the current patterns in the payment for the labor of men and women, she describes the distinct premises on which wages for men and for women have been calculated. In the case of men, the prevailing standard for establishing wages was originally the nature of the work done and latterly the value of that work in a market for labor. In the case of women, however, the payment of wages was linked to the notion of subsistence. Kessler-Harris points out that, for all of his progressive views on the possible role of educated and politically conscious women in a liberal state, John Stuart Mill, at least for the sake of argument, took a somewhat more rigorous stand on the appropriate level of a *living wage* for women. Such a wage

> must be equal to their support, but need not be more than equal to it; the minimum in their case is the pittance absolutely required for the sustenance of one human being. ([1848] 1963, 395.)

This view was, of course, grounded in a quite orthodox position concerning the appropriate role for women in the family. Mill himself was interested in expanding opportunities for women; he saw the tendency to devalue the labor of both earners in a two-earner family as being a pernicious feature of the economic system. He was, nonetheless, pointing to a set of assumptions that have had a powerful impact on thinking about the basis for wages: men are entitled to a wage that fairly represents the market value of the work they do and women should be paid a "living wage" to reflect the fact that if they are working they are not fulfilling their more natural role as homemakers and mothers. This view continues in some respects to influence the wage structure and arguments about the relative wages of male and female workers.

A close relative of the distinction between males' wages being tied to the nature of work, and females' wages to subsistence was the idea of the *family wage*. The reformers and "maternal feminists" of the late nineteenth and early twentieth centuries were demanding that wages reflect a man's responsibility to support a wife and children.[17] These reformers generally agreed that the proper sphere for the activity of women lay in the home; they saw the "profession" of women as that of creating a domestic environment in which healthy and well-adjusted men and children would live. They argued that women could be liberated from their menial and low-paying jobs for this purpose only if their husbands were paid a wage high enough to support families.

This idea of the family wage had a strong influence in the early twentieth century economy. One of its effects, of course, was to legitimize the idea of a living wage for women and to sanction the ghettoization of women in particular kinds of jobs, an effect still evident in wage patterns. Brown, in fact, suggests that the welfare state in the form we currently know it owes much to the collapse of the exchange between wage work in the economy and unpaid work in the home: "unpaid reproductive work continues, and continues being performed primarily by women, even though this work is increasingly (under-)supported by the welfare state rather than by a male wage." (1992, 21).

Equal Pay...Pay Equity

Kessler-Harris (1990) traces the first notion of *equal pay* for women in the United States to the period of World War I. She argues that the interest in equal pay at that point sprang from concern that employers would exploit the opportunity offered by the large numbers of women in the jobs of men absent in the armed forces; the fear was that wages would be lowered, creating hardships for the families of the men when they returned. Thus, the motivation behind the steps taken to pay women the amount

---

17 Much has been written about the maternal feminists and their effect on Canadian public policy concerning employment conditions, temperance, crime, family planning, and numerous other important social issues during this period. See, to cite just one example, Chunn 1988.

men had been paid for the same job was in large part to counteract the depressive effect the presence of women would have on *men's* wages. There is evidence of a parallel concern during World War II.

McDermott (1991a, 21) describes the evolution of this issue in Canada following World War II, a course closely resembling that described by Kessler-Harris for the United States. Whatever the origins of the pressure for equal pay for equal work, the goal was seen in the postwar period as a matter of social justice for female workers. By the end of the 1950s, many Canadian jurisdictions had passed legislation requiring women to be paid wages equivalent to those of men for doing the same job.

This version of pay equity did not, of course, allow any inroads to be made on the part of the male-female wage differential that is explained by the segregation of women in "women's jobs," which have been, almost by definition, lower paid than men's jobs. As part of the wave of antidiscrimination legislation of the 1970s, several jurisdictions, including Quebec and the federal government, passed provisions based on the idea of *equal pay for work of equal value*. These laws allowed human rights commissions to examine a number of components of jobs and to decide whether these components were compensated at the same level for men and women. Marcotte (1987) discusses the example of a complaint made to the Canadian Human Rights Commission concerning the variance in wages between federal government librarians, a majority of whom were men, and historical researchers, who were mostly women. As a result of the examination of the nature of the two jobs, the commission concluded that the complaint lodged on behalf of the researchers was well founded, and adjustments of $479 to $6,300 were made in their annual salaries.

Since the mid-1980s, five provinces[18] have passed equal pay legislation based on the notion of *comparable worth*. Under these

---

18 Manitoba (1985), Ontario (1987), Nova Scotia (1988), Prince Edward Island (1988), and New Brunswick (1989).

statutes, the focus is not on complaints laid by employees or on comparisons between individual jobs but on employers' obligation to examine their own wage structures as a whole for evidence of discriminatory practices and to submit a wage adjustment plan for consideration by a pay equity tribunal.[19]

The Ambiguity of Equality

One of the things any review of the historical legacy reveals is the duality or ambiguity of ideas concerning equality, advantage, and justice in the workplace. Kessler-Harris (1992) and other commentators point out that the platform of pay equity for women, for example, has thrown forth principles that seem inconsistent, advocates who seem to be talking at cross-purposes, and numerous sets of strange bedfellows. Maternal feminists generally saw employment as an unpleasant necessity from which women needed to be freed in order to pursue their proper profession of homemaking. Their view of the liberation of women focused on the primacy of their role within the family. Current feminists see this view as demeaning to women, while acknowledging that the position of women as members, and often supporters, of families must be recognized.

Mandatory Retirement

The same kind of ambiguity exists in relation to mandatory retirement, another issue that is currently receiving much attention. Mandatory retirement, combined with adequate pension entitlements, was an important goal of trade unions and progressive political parties earlier in this century. The liberation of the

---

19 See also *County of Washington v. Gunther* (USSC. 80-429), in which the United States Supreme Court accepted that existing civil rights legislation could accommodate a move away from the equal-pay-for-equal-work standard toward the comparable-worth approach.

older worker from the necessity of continuing to work in order to survive and the provision of resources for a period of leisure with dignity after retirement were seen as an important social achievement. Today, however, some people view mandatory retirement not as a benefit but as a possible violation of constitutional equality. The debate surrounding this transformation demonstrates the ambiguity that may inhere in an issue of this kind. The possibility that an individual worker will be able to challenge mandatory retirement provisions on the grounds that they represent discrimination on the basis of age clearly has a great many significant implications. The issue has obvious relevance to the future structure of pension plans, the retirement provisions of collective agreements, the job opportunities for workers entering the labor market, the standards of assessment for work performance, and the right of employers to demand performance and to dismiss for cause. Some also argue it raises the specter of older workers "being deprived of the choice of a leisurely retirement, as pension plans are reorganized to reflect the assumption that workers will be working to a later point in their lives.[20]

A number of writers who have directed their attention to the policy issues surrounding mandatory retirement (Adams 1992; Gunderson and Pesando 1988) point out that the question of what is in the best interest of older workers and what represents fair treatment for them is one that cannot be accurately answered by a simplistic assertion of formal equality of an individualistic kind. Though Krashinsky (1988) seems to equate the protection of equality under section 15 of the Charter with the abolition of mandatory retirement, he does acknowledge that other factors enter into the equation.

In the *McKinney* case,[21] the judges of the Supreme Court of Canada wrestled with the significance of mandatory retirement

20 John Kettle (1993) suggests that this may occur, in any case, as the effect of a decline in the health of pension funds.

21 *McKinney v. Board of Governors of the University of Guelph* (1991), 76 DLR (4th) 545.

vis-à-vis the guarantee of equality in the Charter. This particular challenge to mandatory retirement arose in the somewhat specialized environment of the university,[22] but the decision is nonetheless illustrative of the ambiguous implications of this issue.

The question was whether the provisions of the Human Rights Code of Ontario, in which the proscription of discrimination on the basis of age was limited to the ages between 18 and 65 years, were inconsistent with section 15 of the Charter. The majority of the justices concluded that, although the legislation did constitute a violation of section 15, it was rescued by section 1, which guarantees the rights and freedoms set out in the Charter "subject only to such reasonable limits prescribed by law as can be demonstrably justified in a free and democratic society."

The members of the court who agreed that the impingement on equality represented by mandatory retirement was "demonstrably justified" examined a wide variety of issues. In his judgment, Mr. Justice Gerald LaForest stated:

> What we are confronted with is a complex socio-economic problem that involves the basic and interconnected rules of the workplace throughout the whole of our society. As already mentioned, the legislature was not operating in a vacuum. Mandatory retirement has long been with us; it is widespread throughout the labour market; it involves 50% of the workforce. The legislature's concerns were with the ramifications of changing what had for long been the rule on such important social issues as its effect on pension plans, youth employment, the desirability of those in the workplace to bargain for and organize their own terms of employment, the advantages flowing from expectations and ongoing arrangements about

---

22 Indeed, it should be noted that four members of the majority of the Court subscribed to the view that universities are not part of the apparatus of government and that, therefore, the protection of equality under section 15 does not apply as such to them. This way of thinking does not, of course, mean that universities would be free to discriminate on whatever basis they like — provincial human rights legislation prohibits this — but it does mean that the guarantee of equality would not apply in its full constitutional force.

> terms of employment, including not only retirement, but
> seniority and tenure and, indeed, almost every aspect of the
> employer-employee relationship. (*McKinney*, 664.)

In two dissenting judgments, Madam Justices Bertha Wilson and Claire L'Heureux-Dubé stated their view that the impugned provision of the Ontario legislation and the mandatory retirement system that it permits do constitute a violation of the guarantee of equality in the Charter. As Madam Justice Wilson put it, to allow the enforcement of mandatory retirement was to reinforce the stereotype that "with age comes increasing incompetence and decreasing intellectual capacity" (ibid., 610). In her view, older workers are entitled to protection from affronts to their dignity and assaults on their interests resting on such prejudicial assumptions.

Double Meanings:
A Search for Solutions

When closely scrutinized, the issue of mandatory retirement, like that of equal pay, reveals a double meaning in terms of discrimination against older workers and women. Does mandatory retirement protect older workers by making it possible for them to withdraw from the labor force with a secure income, or is it an affront to their independence and dignity? Do the wages of women reflect a respect for the family as an economic and social unit or a means of discouraging women from taking a fully equal role in the workforce?

The significance of such questions for the formulation of social policy is clearly enormous, and it is impossible here to provide comprehensive answers to them. It seems to me, however, that one of the reasons the alternatives — those before the court in the *McKinney* case, for example — seem so extreme is that the value put on paid work in society is equated with the value of the individual to society.

Canadian social policies must find more imaginative ways of approaching the conundrum of providing for the financial, social, and intellectual needs of members of society in the context of a wage economy. It is likely, for example, that women will continue to play a unique role in the rearing of children, even in two-parent families. As we have seen, the rationale for the differential for female wages has often been based on factors connected with this role — absences from the workforce for childbearing and child-rearing, lack of commitment to a career, a lack or atrophy of requisite skills, and a preference for part-time employment. Yet, as we have also seen, at least part of the differential is based on assumptions about the suitability of women for employment, about their actual or potential family commitments, and about their skills and abilities, which set up an additional barrier to their equitable participation in the workforce.

Women are indeed likely to absent themselves from the workforce for periods of time to pursue family obligations. The natural consequence of these absences is that women may have lower lifetime earnings than men. It is appropriate that significant financial hardship that results should be addressed as a general issue of public policy. What does not seem appropriate in any way is that, in addition to losing income because they are not working, women should be additionally penalized for choosing to be absent. As a result of a decision to take time out of the workforce, women may face barriers to promotion, restrictions on their ability to continue to make contributions to pension or other benefit plans, negative characterizations of their work ethic, and other limitations to their employment or advancement. In many cases, these impediments do not arise from a demonstrable loss of skill or a fair assessment of accrued experience but simply from conformity to an inflexible notion of what constitutes an appropriate career path.

It should surely be possible for policymakers to better accommodate all of these values, which are so often seen as conflicting. It should be possible to provide women with opportunities to nurture their families without foreclosing their legitimate career aspirations or plunging their families into financial crisis. Doing so may require judicious use of resources of governments, of employers, and of individuals themselves. It may require imaginative work scheduling, access to part-time work or job sharing, intermittent or overlapping social assistance, government-employer cooperation on child care facilities, and a variety of other things. But it should be possible.

In the *McKinney* case, the Supreme Court came to a decision that was entirely understandable given the framework of issues it had been presented with and the factual situations it considered. The choice, to put it somewhat simplistically, seemed to be either to allow individuals to go on working past normal retirement age, putting at risk both their own financial security in old age and career opportunities for younger workers, or to sever retirement-age employees from opportunities to continue to contribute their accrued skill and experience and to spend a financially secure old age in constructive and fulfilling activity. The choices are, of course, considerably more nuanced than that. Though the removal of mandatory retirement might play havoc with the current standard assumptions of pension plans, there is no reason such plans could not be adjusted to reflect changed assumptions. Concern about pressure on older workers to stay in the work force need not lead to the institution of "mandatory nonretirement."

Again, it must surely be possible to arrive at a policy solution that takes into account all of the interests alluded to in both the majority and minority decisions of the Supreme Court. There must be some way to avoid the affront to the dignity of older workers implicit in their forced removal from the employment scene — and by implication their value as members of society — without either consigning them to penury or eclipsing the prospects of the young. More flexible pension arrangements, scaled-down working arrangements for older workers, alternative unwaged opportunities to make a contribution — all might be considered in developing policy solutions that are not defined in terms of an absolute discontinuity between employment and retirement. If the objective is equity, the means to that end need not be the same in all cases.

The Pluralistic Nature of Equality

It should be clear that more than one kind of equality is in question. Indeed, the same situation may raise the issue of equality in several different ways.

In the judgment of Madam Justice Wilson in the *McKinney* case, for example, she alludes to the possibility of a double disadvantage for older workers who are also women:

> The statistics show that women workers generally are unable to amass adequate pension earnings during their working years because of the high incidence of interrupted work histories due to child-bearing and child-rearing. Thus, the imposition of mandatory retirement raises not only issues of age discrimination but also may implicate other s. 15 rights as well. (*McKinney*, 627.)

To complicate matters further, she suggests that another source of disadvantage may be the relatively low degree of unionization of certain groups of workers:

> The evidence has established that there is a very high corre-lation between the existence of such pension plans and un-ionization. But the statistics show that the vast proportion of the workforce is unorganized. The preservation of pension schemes has therefore very little relevance in the case of the majority of working people in Ontario. This problem is exac-erbated when the demographics of this portion of the work-force is examined. Immigrant and female labour and the unskilled comprise a disproportionately high percentage of unorganized workers. This group represents the most vulner-able employees. They are the ones who, if forced to retire at

age 65, will be hardest hit by the lack of legislative protection. (Ibid., 626.)

We know relatively little about the interplay between various kinds of discrimination or about how progress toward equality according to one set of criteria affects the possibility of equity for other disadvantaged groups. One calculation based on Canadian median salary data (Weiner 1993) puts the cost of being a woman at $8,429 annually and the cost of being black and a woman at $10,264. Whether or not these particular figures are accurate, they are an example of a shift from thinking of equality as a monolithic concept to a recognition that it must be analyzed a differentiated way.

One of the most difficult things that Canadian feminists have had to come to terms with is their increasing conviction that the returns of any modest progress made toward equitable terms and conditions of employment have gone disproportionately to well-educated, articulate, white, middle-class women — at the expense of those who lie on the other side of distinctions based on race, disability, or class. Bakker (1991, 271) describes a trend in the past few years to a polarization of earnings. At one end of the scale, workers, including an increasing number of women, have gravitated toward stable, well-paid jobs; the other, nonstandard end of the spectrum is characterized by lower and more erratic earnings. Unless we better understand the effect of what Weiner (1993) refers to as double or triple jeopardy — that is, the interplay of several possible sources of disadvantage — it is difficult to see how effective steps can be taken toward true equity in employment.

Conclusion

In a recent article, Yves-Marie Morissette argues that the entrenchment of rights in the Charter and the quasi-constitutional status of related provisions in human rights legislation do not accord well with Canadian social and political traditions:

Between the two extremes of too much law (as in the United States) and not enough law (as in Japan), Canada had achieved a workable compromise. This compromise is now in jeopardy. The U.S. has such a terribly weak social security net that we can readily see why people eventually use rights to force redistributions. Many children born in the urban ghettos of this Haven of Rights continue to live thoroughly Hobbesian lives — solitary, poor, nasty, brutish and short. Individual rights are not what will help them. We Canadians appear to have understood that for most of our national history; thus our social-security net. In a society like Japan, the weight of social convention prevents the growth of law. Ultimately, the law loses its purpose. Such a society curtails individualism to an extent we Canadians would not tolerate. Sameness is far from being a dominant characteristic of our country.

We must therefore maintain a middle course between communitarian good and individualism. (1994, 154.)

I argued earlier that the model of rights-based adjudication can be indicative of firmly held national values, but there is something to Professor Morissette's comment that the language of these provisions is more of a rhetorical and ideological piece with the individualistic and libertarian disposition of US polity than with the pragmatic and collaborative approach that has been more common in Canada. Obsession, as he rightly suggests, can be a dangerous element in national policy.

One of the most sensitive tasks for an administrative agency charged with providing support for the principle of equity must surely be that of deciding when collective interests should have priority over individual claims and what role the flourishing individual has in creating a strong community. These determinations have not been made any less difficult in Canada by a formulation of the issues that characterizes those who argue the need for specific mechanisms to redress inequities as representatives of special interest groups. By framing the argument in this way, those who oppose such interventionist policies are able, in an odd sense, to claim the communitarian ground as their own and to label the seekers of protection as the ones who are selfish and unfair.

The kinds of legal and administrative structures I have discussed are based, I think, on a slightly different set of assumptions — namely, that "special interest groups" are so disadvantaged that they cannot hold their own in a simple majoritarian structure and that steps taken to secure substantive equality for these groups are for the good of the whole community, not just for the members of the vulnerable groups themselves.

The extent to which we as a collectivity are justified in restricting the initiative or aggrandizement of individuals in order to repair the fortunes of the weak or disadvantaged is clearly a matter that has been and will be productive of infinite debate. As Professor Morissette intimates, however, an ethos of collective responsibility is not foreign to Canadian policymaking or, I suggest, indigestible for Canadian administrative agencies.

As I pointed out at the outset of this paper, Canadians have tended to approach the making of policy in a constructively pragmatic way. As Professor Morissette suggests, we as a society have not accepted that the primacy of rights for individuals should be pressed to the point at which the vulnerable are consumed as a result of some sort of Darwinian logic. Though the rhetoric of the Charter echoes the rights-based assumptions of US constitutional tradition, the Charter itself must be seen as part of a web of constitutional and legislative provisions, administrative mechanisms, and historical tradition that give it a resonance distinct from that of the US bill of rights. Our legal institutions, our administrative tribunals, and our policymakers operate in a peculiarly Canadian environment in which the rights enshrined in the Charter are only one element and in which the balancing of collective and individual interests is a familiar exercise.

In the passage quoted above, Professor Morissette seems to use *law* — as in "too much law" — to refer particularly to the mediation of the claims of individuals through the judicial system. In my view, law is a more pervasive concept, one that includes the activities of legislatures and of the administrative bodies through which those legislatures effect the public policies they wish to advance. In this sense, law is the means by which public interests and public obligations are factored into a consideration of particular claims or allegations. Though there may well be a danger of "too much law" in the sense Professor Morissette means — the pursuit of rights-based claims to the detriment of other legitimate public objectives — the law as I understand it plays a pervasive and necessary role in setting public priorities and weighing the value of particular claims or policies.

In a recent paper, economist Judith Maxwell (1994) argues that current economic features, such as large public debt, technological change, and the forces of global trade, have created pressures and dangers in the workplace that can be addressed only if Canadian policymakers adopt a holistic approach that takes into account the interconnections of the workplace, the community, the family, and other social institutions. The workplace cannot sensibly be viewed as a separate sphere in which displacement of workers or changes in the nature and quantity of the work they do will not have repercussions in the outside world.

In this holistic universe, the calls of those claiming equity do not become irrelevant, and they should not be silenced. The need is more pressing than ever for a legal framework that makes provision for continued support of the legitimate aspirations of those for whom equity has not yet been achieved. The goal of equity is not a peripheral aspiration that should be put aside until we have more money or more time or less controversy. It is a central idea in a democratic society and one that merits our attention.

References

Abella, Rosalie S. 1987. "The Social and Legal Paradigms of Equality." *Windsor Review of Social and Legal Issues* 1: 5–16.

Adams, George W. 1992. *Mandatory Retirement and Constitutional Choices*. Current Issues Series. Kingston, Ont.: Queen's University, Industrial Relations Centre.

Aldrich, Mark, and Robert Buchele, eds. 1986. *The Economics of Comparable Work*. Cambridge, Mass.: Ballinger.

Brown, Wendy. 1992. "Finding the Man in the State." *Feminist Studies* 18: 7–22.

Bakker, Isabella. 1991. "Pay Equity and Economic Restructuring: The Polarization of Policy?" In Judy Fudge and Patricia McDermott, eds., *Just Wages: A Feminist Assessment of Pay Equity*. Toronto: University of Toronto Press.

Chunn, Dorothy. 1988. "Maternal Feminism, Legal Professionalism and Political Pragmatism: The Rise and Fall of Magistrate Margaret Patterson, 1922–34." In W. Wesley Pue and Barry Wright, eds., *Canadian Perspectives on Law and Society: Issues in Legal History*. Ottawa: Carleton University Press.

Courchene, Thomas J. 1987. *Social Policy in the 1990s: Agenda for Reform*. Policy Study 3. Toronto: C.D. Howe Institute.

———. 1994. *Social Canada in the Millennium: Reform Imperatives and Restructuring Principles*. The Social Policy Challenge 4. Toronto: C.D. Howe Institute.

England, Paula. 1992. *Comparable Worth: Theories and Evidence*. New York: Aldine de Gruyter.

Fudge, Judy, and Patricia McDermott, eds. 1991. *Just Wages: A Feminist Assessment of Pay Equity*. Toronto: University of Toronto Press.

Gunderson, Morley, and James Pesando. 1988. "The Case for Allowing Mandatory Retirement." *Canadian Public Policy* 14: 32–39.

Kessler-Harris, Alice. 1990. *A Woman's Wage: Historical Meanings and Social Consequences*. Lexington, Ky.: University Press of Kentucky.

Kettle, John. 1993. "When You Reach Age 65, Don't Be Surprised If You're Too Young to Retire." *Globe and Mail* (Toronto), October 21.

Krashinsky, Michael. 1988. "The Case for Eliminating Mandatory Retirement: Why Economics and Human Rights Need Not Conflict." *Canadian Public Policy* 14: 40–51.

McDermott, Patricia. 1991a. "Pay Equity in Canada: Assessing the Commitment to Reducing the Wage Gap." In Judy Fudge and patricia McDermott, eds., *Just Wages: A Feminist Assessment of Pay Equity*. Toronto: University of Toronto Press.

————. 1991b. "The Pay Equity Challenge to Collective Bargaining in Ontario." In Judy Fudge and Patricia McDermott, eds., *Just Wages: A Feminist View of Pay Equity*. Toronto: University of Toronto Press.

Marcotte, Marilee. 1987. *Equal Pay for Work of Equal Value*. Kingston, Ont.: Queen's University, Industrial Relations Center.

Maxwell, Judith. 1994. "Economic Insecurity and the Labour Market." Keynote address to the 12th annual Labour Arbitration Conference, Calgary, Alberta, May 25.

Mill, John Stuart. [1848] 1963. *Principles of Political Economy with Some of Their Applications to Social Philosophy*. Edited by J.M. Robson. Vol. 2 of *Collected Works of J.S. Mill*, 33 v. Toronto: University of Toronto Press.

Morissette, Yves-Marie. 1994. "Canada as a Post-Modern Kritarchy: Or Why Should Judges Make Political Decisions." *Inroads* 3: 144–155.

Ontario. 1984. Royal Commission on Equity and Employment. *Report*. Toronto: Government of Ontario Chair was Madam Justice Rosalie Abella.

Robb, Roberta Edgecombe. 1987. "Equal Pay for Work of Equal Value: Issues and Policies." *Canadian Public Policy* 13: 445–461.

Sorensen, Elaine. 1991. *Exploring the Reasons behind the Narrowing Gender Gap in Earnings*. Washington, DC: Urban Institute Press.

Treiman, Donald J. and Heidi I. Hartmann, eds. 1981. *Women, Work and Wages: Equal Pay for Jobs of Equal Value*. Washington, DC: National Academy Press.

Weiner, Nan. 1993. "Employment Equity and Pay Equity: Similarities, Differences and Integration," *Canadian Labour Law Journal* 2: 16–31.

A Comment

Roger Phillips

My reflections on the three papers in this volume are based not on academic research but on instincts and experience accumulated over a business career of 35 years. That career has seen me closely involved in industrial relations since the early 1960s. It has embroiled me in several important industrial relations innovations, and for part of the time it permitted me a window on labor issues outside North America — in Europe, in particular.

I have read with interest the three papers in this volume. I begin with Roy Adams' contrast between "social partnership" and "adversarial" nations.

In two tables, Adams compares the performance of seven "partnership" countries and seven "adversarial" ones. The data cover two overlapping periods, 1970–92 and 1983–92. On average, the partnership countries enjoyed slightly higher growth of gross domestic product (GDP), slightly lower inflation, considerably lower unemployment, and much lower strike rates. But there are problems with averages constructed over periods of several decades. One is that they can hide trends: Sweden, for example, fared much worse toward the end of this period than at the beginning. Another problem with the data used by Adams is that they ignore measures of real per capita GDP, and yet by this criterion the adversarial group fares much better.

Whereas the 1970–92 period may be too long for some kinds of analysis, for others it may be too short. We must ask the question: Are we looking for a system that can work well over 20 years or over 100? This is an important question when we are assessing large institutions, such as industrial relations systems, that possess great inertia. No system works perfectly; some slight fault may lead to severe long-term problems. To use a mathematical analogy, suppose one system gets industrial relations "right" 95 percent of the time, but when it gets matters "wrong," society suffers severely. Meanwhile another system gets it right only 80 percent of the time, but when matters go wrong, society suffers much less than under the first system. Which system is preferable? After 22 years, the probability that the first system will have got it right every year is 32 percent ($= 0.95^{22}$); under the second system, the probability that things will have gone right every year is below 1 percent ($= 0.8^{22}$). But it may well be preferable to adopt the second system and incur a higher probability that matters will go wrong, since going wrong under the first system entails such severe shocks to society. What we should be looking for is not necessarily the system with the highest probability of getting it right over a particular period, but one whose deficiencies will not lead to major crises.

The Swedish model is an example of the first system. For many years, Swedish labor relations worked well, but when a series of strikes in 1990 signaled serious social conflicts, the system could not adapt. I concur with those observers who argue that the seeds of its destruction had been sown long before. It attempted to maintain taxes at an unsustainably high level and created too many disincentives against productive investment and employment. The Swedish model has gone dramatically "wrong" in the post-1990 recession; it has produced major political traumas that remain unhealed.

Foreign critics could hardly be more severe than the Swedish government itself when it comes to describing that country's economic problems this decade. Here are excerpts from a recent (November 1994) official publication:

> For many years, Sweden has had one of the highest labor market participation rates in the world. While unemployment in other countries continued to mount after the oil crises of the 1970s, Sweden remained a sterling exception. The

percentage of the population aged 16–64 with paid jobs rose sharply from about 70 percent in the early 1950s to 82.6 percent in 1990. The continuous expansion of the public sector is one important reason for this trend. Since 1950 all employment growth has taken place in the public sector.

So far during the 1990s, the situation in the labor market has drastically changed. Sweden's lead has vanished. Between 1990 and 1993 the labor force shrank by about 500,000 people. As a result, the participation rate among people aged 16–64 slid to 72.6 percent.

The fall in gainful employment resulted in a dramatically higher jobless rate. In 1993 registered unemployment totaled 8.2 percent compared with 1.7 percent in 1990 [or with the 2.3 percent average reported by Adams for the 1970–92 period]. The increase in registered unemployment was far less than the decline in employment, however, because many people who lost their jobs entered labor market programs, became students or began collecting disability pensions...

The recession of the past few years has led to a dramatic worsening of government finances. Tax revenues have declined while expenditures have risen sharply. In 1989 Sweden's public sector showed a financial surplus equivalent to 5.4 percent of GDP, the largest among the members of the Organisation for Economic Co-operation and Development (OECD). By 1993 it was showing a deficit of 13.4 percent of GDP, the largest among the OECD countries.

This sharp deterioration in government finances was one important factor behind the growing lack of confidence in the Swedish krona late in the summer of 1992. By autumn, the situation became acute. Sweden's non-socialist coalition Government joined forces with the largest opposition party, the Social Democrats, to develop a reform package aimed at improving public finances. It included higher excise taxes and lower transfer payments to households. (Swedish Institute 1994, 3.)

Despite such reform packages, Sweden has yet to make much progress in cutting the public sector deficit. At 59 percent, Swedish government spending relative to GDP was already very high in 1990. This ratio peaked at 73 percent in 1993, and for 1995 it is projected to be 68 percent. The Social Democrats were in office when the recession began. Their attempts to exercise fiscal restraint proved unpopular, and they were replaced in 1991 by a Conservative government. It, in turn, had limited success in reducing the deficit. Swedish dissatisfaction with the Conservatives resulted in a return to office in 1994 of the Social Democrats, but the fiscal problems remain. Sweden's deficit was 10 percent for 1994 and is projected at 9 percent for 1995 (OECD 1995, tables 28,30). In 1990, Sweden's net public sector debt was a respectable 44 percent of GDP. By the end of 1995, Sweden's public sector debt-to-GDP ratio is forecast to be above 100 percent — which means Sweden will have exceeded Canada's dismal debt record. As a model for Canada, Sweden is, I conclude, inappropriate, and I shall give it no further discussion here.

The Japanese system has also started to destroy itself, albeit not to the same extent as Sweden's. For example, the costly promise of jobs for life in the steel industry worked when Japan boasted the world's most productive steel producers. But this promise has now become a severe impediment to Japan's ability to compete internationally. From the lowest-cost steel and auto producer, Japan has become one of the most expensive. Once able to count on a buoyant internal market at higher-than-world prices, Japanese steel producers now suffer from a weakened domestic market made all the weaker by their two-price system. This is but one example of a faltering Japanese economy. Taken on its own, it does not allow us to disregard the Japanese experience, but the substantial cultural differences separating Japan and Canada would make the adoption of Japanese industrial relations extremely difficult.

Accordingly, I restrict further comment to comparisons among Canada, the United States, and Germany. First, let us review Adams' data for the 1983–92 period. In Table 1, I have added columns showing per capita GDP and current unemployment rates.

With the exception of days lost to industrial conflict, there was little difference between United States and Germany over the decade in review. Growth was somewhat slower in the United

Table 1: *Selected Socio-Economic Indicators,*
Canada, United States, and Germany, 1983–92

	Canada	United States	Germany
Per capita GDP, 1992 (1987 US$)	16,208	19,519	17,731
Per capita GDP growth (%)	2.5	2.7	3.0
Inflation rate (%)	4.4	3.8	2.2
Unemployment rate (%)	9.6	6.7	6.8
Unemployment rate, June 1995 (%)	9.6	5.6	8.3
Days lost to industrial conflict (per 1,000 workers)	345	76	29

Note: Annual averages unless otherwise indicated.

Source: *The Economist* 1995.

States than in Germany, but US economic well-being, as expressed in per capita GDP, was still 10 percent higher in 1992. Inflation was somewhat higher in the United States than in Germany, but unemployment was marginally lower. By these criteria, the "adversarial" United States is currently performing better than "partnership" Germany.

Readers should be careful in interpreting strike data. Such statistics are frequently inaccurate, and international comparisons are extremely hard to make. A prolonged strike in a crucial sector (for example, the British coal miners' strike in 1984–85) can cause far more economic disruption than one-day nation-wide political strikes called by union centrals in countries such as Italy. But the latter may generate more days lost than the former. Let me discuss my own experience.

In early 1981, I became interested in unauthorized absenteeism among workers in the principal countries in which my then employer owned factories. To my surprise, by far the highest absentee rate was in West Germany, substantially ahead of Canada, the United States, and "strike-ridden" Britain! How could the contradiction between these absenteeism statistics and Germany's reputation for peaceful labor relations be reconciled? To my inquiries, German managers replied: "That's easily explained. These absentees are engaged in 'personal strikes'." In the German labor relations model, top union officials in a centralized collective bargaining system make deals with their counterparts in employer federations and government. Individual workers feel left out. With no other way to express their own workplace concerns, employees resort to unauthorized absences — which are never recorded as strikes — as a way of letting off steam. It is a practice so prevalent that, as noted above, my German colleagues had a name for it.

This anecdotal evidence suggests to me that "days lost to industrial conflict and unauthorized absenteeism" would be a far better measure of social stability. Meanwhile, I can only conclude that the apparent industrial peace in Germany is misleading, and readers should treat such data with caution.

Adams makes a revealing comment in his discussion of pattern bargaining in Germany that lends credence to my view that the German worker may not feel well served by the "social partnership" he extols. "Most German unions," Adams says, "being poorly organized on the shop floor..., have a difficult time putting a convincing case for union membership to the nonunionist." In recent years the metalworkers' union, whose centralized negotiations have usually set the pattern for wage increases, has had a less cozy arrangement with employers than earlier. Its leaders have been listening more closely to workers' immediate concerns and have been paying less attention to the longer term. The result has been more aggressive bargaining, wage increases, and changes in work rules whose costs have outstripped productivity improvements. The result is not altogether favorable for German workers. This more aggressive bargaining has contributed to a rise in unemployment. At 8.3 percent in June 1995, German unemployment is, like Sweden's, well above the average reported by Adams.

Table 2: *Selected Socio-Economic Indicators,*
United States and Germany, 1970–92

	Per Capita GDP Growth	Inflation Rate	Unemploy-ment Rate	Days Lost to Industrial Conflict
	(%)	(%)	(%)	*(per 1,000 workers)*
1970–82				
United States	1.1	10.6	6.5	305.0
Germany	4.6	5.0	2.9	35.1
1983–92				
United States	2.7	3.8	6.7	75.7
Germany	3.0	2.2	6.8	28.9

Note: Data are annual averages.

Source: Adams, in this volume.

While it is too early to read the last rites for Germany's social partnership model, it seems fair to conclude that a consensual system between the elites of labor and employers bought early economic successes but could not succeed in the long run. The workers' dissatisfaction grew, and the economy developed systemic rigidities; the combined effect has been to eat away at overall German efficiency. I illustrate this conclusion in Table 2, where I have rearranged Adams' data for Germany and the United States to show the change between the first and second halves of his 1970–92 period.

A comparison of the first and second ranges shows convergence among all four variables. The German growth rate declined; in the United States, growth accelerated. German inflation declined; US inflation declined even more. Average US unemployment was nearly constant; German unemployment caught up. Finally, the strike data show a precipitate decline in the United States, albeit — if you believe the data — Germany still loses much less time to strikes. Add anecdotal evidence, such as Mercedes-

Benz starting to produce cars in the United States, and instinc-tively one has to conclude that all is not right in Germany.

While cynics may conclude that both Adams and I have merely proved the adage "liars sure can figure," a more reason-able conclusion is that caution is needed. In the longer term, it is not at all certain that the most successful "social partnerships" can beat out the most successful "adversarial" countries.

While I am skeptical of Adams' conclusion, I do not want to dismiss the value of international comparisons. Nor should we reject another message from his numbers: compared with the United States, Canada has a poor record. Over the 1983–92 period, Canada had lower per capita GDP growth than the United States (2.5 percent compared with 2.7 percent), higher unemploy-ment (9.6 percent versus 6.7 percent), and higher inflation (4.4 per-cent versus 3.8 percent). Industrial conflict in Canada, as measured by days lost per thousand workers, is tops among the members of the OECD, and is nothing short of scandalous. I shall return to these problems later.

Gordon Betcherman's essay is the most interesting of the trilogy in that it breaks new ground. He is exploring an important question: what are the relationships between management strate-gies and the changing nature of employment? I suspect, however, that Betcherman's essay is just a beginning, and that there will be many more inquiries into the relation between internal and external labor markets. I am instinctively suspicious of conclu-sions based on written surveys, but my chief concern with Betcher-man's essay is some apparent contradictions in his analysis.[1]

---

1 Hardly a week goes by during which, in my role as a chief executive officer at IPSCO, I do not receive one or more surveys being conducted by think tanks, university academics, or graduate students. The surveys are always accom-panied by polite covering letters that assure us simultaneously that the results will be of extreme academic importance and yet that the questionnaire will take only a few minutes to complete. Most secretaries intercept these requests before they reach the chief executive officer and refer them instead to some appropriate vice-president whose secretary in turn passes the task of completing the form to a hapless staff member. For ease of analysis, the surveys frequently use scales (for example, "how innovative are your firm's...

He makes assumptions with respect to commitment between employer and employee and the nature of work in modern, computer-based production facilities for which I cannot find justification in his paper — and which I doubt to be correct. For one, he believes that European "cooperative" systems engender employee commitment. This I discuss later. For another, he states that "[t]he potential of computer-based production could only be fully exploited through flexible specialization," which meant "less rigid workplace practices than were typical of the traditional blue-collar system." In fact, however, computer-based production requires much more rigid adherence to predetermined standard operating procedures, and it has done away with the individualized "black art" of traditional factory machine operators. Only imperfectly understood by management, this black art allowed the workers considerable autonomy under traditional work organization.

The all-encompassing nature of Betcherman's categories poses further problems. Trying to fit all internal labor markets (ILMs) into one of three models is too much of a stretch. Within any one firm, there may well be different ILM models. For instance, in fabricated metal products firms, one model will exist on the factory floor, another among middle management, a third among technical employees (such as engineering, research, and metallurgy), and a fourth among senior management. To compli-

---

Note 1 - cont'd.

...hiring practices: very innovative, sophisticated, normal, conservative?"). The hapless employee filling in the blanks may attempt to guess how the more senior officer would have answered, or may substitute his or her own views, or may decide to answer in a way that makes the firm look good. Certainly, I would be highly suspicious of any conclusions drawn from responses to the above example. In general, research based on written questionnaires is unsatisfactory and leads to misleading results. To have any validity, a skilled interviewer who is involved academically in the particular research should conduct an oral interview of an hour or more, preferably with several people in any firm being surveyed. My own practice is *not* to delegate the completion of such questionnaires to subordinates. I always read the documents, if only to determine what the current business research fad is. Then I write back, enclosing the uncompleted questionnaire, and explain why I believe the methodology to be faulty.

cate matters further, a firm with multiple plants may well use different ILM models at different plants.

Betcherman begins by documenting certain undeniable and disturbing trends. Canadian unemployment rates have risen dramatically since the Second World War. For any stage in the business cycle, they are higher now than one or two generations ago. Furthermore, unemployment among primary workers and long-term unemployment have both increased. For those who believe in social equity, it is disconcerting that full-time, full-year earnings have grown more polarized and that young workers are faring worse in this decade than young workers did in previous decades. While these trends are clearly undesirable, it is less clear that growth in "nonstandard" employment is equally undesirable. In assessing nonstandard employment, the basic question is whether it is due to broad economic and social changes and is what the workers want, or whether it is an imposition by employers that helps explain undesirable trends.

Let me first examine what Betcherman defines as the "traditional" Canadian ILM:

> Organizations in this cluster are characterized by: conventional (that is, Taylorist) job designs; limited employee participation in the operation of the work unit or organization; "straight" compensation systems (that is, without incentive-based features); little or no training; no flexible scheduling arrangements; and little integration of human resource issues in overall business planning.

I suggest that this definition describes quite well the preponderant ILM form in the countries he cites — in the lower-left quadrant of his Figure 6 — as having social and labor policies and institutions that foster high commitment between employer and employee. (For the purposes of this argument, I shall concern myself with factory-based manufacturing comparisons.) These countries operate ILMs with conventional job design, little participation by employees in the operation of the work unit, straight compensation systems (Japan excepted), and only minimal flexible scheduling arrangements. Some will claim that the institutionalized involvement of unions in business management in most of these countries means high participation by employees. As I have argued with respect to Adams, however, this is not the case.

One possible difference between the European ILM models and more traditional Canadian models is workplace training. I believe that here, too, appearances are deceiving. In Europe, the high level of job tenure seems to be due to employment laws that have made short-term layoffs economically costly for the employer and hence less prevalent. In contrast, the seasonal nature of many Canadian sectors, combined with an unemployment insurance system that subsidizes seasonal employment, means that the traditional Canadian ILM entails lower average tenure on the job. What do European employers do with workers idled by business recessions but still employed because of high severance costs? The answer: set up training courses. Thus, the OECD comment quoted by Betcherman, "Training increases with employment stability," could be rewritten, "Legislation creates employment stability, which in turn induces firms to set up training for otherwise idle workers during recessions." I conclude from my observations of European steel operations that much of this training is highly institutionalized and bureaucratic, and that analysts make the all-too-frequent error of failing to evaluate the results of the training. More training is useful only if it generates more productivity among trained workers.

One of the contradictions of Betcherman's essay is that he may be describing nonexistent differences. In the countries in the lower left quadrant of his Figure 6, the ILMs at the factory level are similar to those in Canada. In explaining differences in job tenure, we must look to factors other than the kinds of ILMs (which are similar) or alleged differences in "employee commitment," a difference he asserts but does not demonstrate. Betcherman admits one significant disadvantage of long job tenure among "standard" employees — namely, high levels of long-term unemployment. A European worker is either in or out. Given the high costs of layoffs in Europe, firms are reluctant to take on new workers during economic booms for fear of the financial implications in a subsequent recession.

Let us turn now to Betcherman's two nontraditional ILMs.

The first, which he terms compensation based, is defined by the use of extrinsic rewards to induce productivity. Firms using this model have sophisticated compensation systems with incentive payments, above-average wages, extensive benefits, and a tendency to promote from within. Betcherman says that firms in this category are disproportionately "large establishments" and disproportionately in the business services sector. This clue leads me to believe that most "compensation-based ILMs" are simply large, bureaucratically organized financial institutions. They employ complex pay and reward schemes linked to short-term profits. But whether these schemes are genuinely increasing economic productivity is open to doubt. My skepticism is not intended to deny the existence of some real cases of innovative compensation-based ILMs. Genuine productivity-enhancing examples of compensation-based ILMs are probably to be found primarily in small, not large, establishments.

The other nontraditional ILM Betcherman describes is the participation-based model, which emphasizes mainly intrinsic rewards to motivate employees. I believe further study will reveal that most firms that use intrinsic rewards are simultaneously using compensation-based rewards. Firms found to be using this model are disproportionately mid-sized establishments (with 100 to 249 employees), electrical- and electronic-product firms, and firms that had experienced a high level of technological change and reorganization over the preceding five years. In short, these are newer firms in expanding market sectors. They are often firms whose products have a short life and in sectors where new firms are being created daily and existing firms are biting the dust at a similar rate. (The latter do not answer questionnaires on optimal ILM models.)

In conclusion, Betcherman is onto something. Nontraditional ILMs are arising among growing firms in an increasingly competitive world. When these ILMs allow better overall service to customers at lower cost, traditionally managed firms will be crowded out. A good example is in the North American steel industry, where nontraditionally managed "mini-mills" are growing in relative market share compared with traditional "integrated" steel companies.

While I have faulted some of the logic of both Adams and Betcherman, each is addressing undeniably important socioeconomic problems facing Canada. Both refer to our high unemployment, and Adams fingers the large amount of work time lost to industrial conflict. By contrast, Beth Bilson addresses a much more nebulous problem — workplace equity. High unemployment and industrial conflict clearly hurt the overall economy. For example, the cost of unemployment extends beyond the idled workers; the cost of work stoppages extends beyond the firms involved in any dispute. But the costs imposed by a lack of workplace equity are far harder to quantify. While one can argue that, in a society truly without discrimination, the economy would be more productive, equity is primarily a distributional and moral problem. Bilson confirms this in stating that she "is concerned only with policies related to the terms and conditions of employment, and other structures in the workplace itself, not with policies related to job creation or the stimulation of regional employment."

Though she addresses many issues, much of her discussion is dominated by male-female equity. My experience with this issue goes back to my earliest years in business. In 1960 my employer had two wage scales, the "M scale" for men and the "F scale" for women. Identical jobs were paid less when performed by women than by men. For example, an Engineer Grade 15M received more than his female counterpart, an Engineer Grade 15F. At the same time, the union contract stipulated that female factory workers receive less for identical jobs, and the union heatedly insisted on maintaining the differential. Times have changed, and equal pay for equal work is a universally accepted principle in Canada.

But the current goal of those who advocate equity is the more complex one of equal pay for work of equal value, where the value is defined to mean something intrinsic to the work and different from market value. Proponents of this goal argue that firms perpetuate systematic discrimination between the pay levels for groups of jobs dominated by men and others dominated by women. The alleged solution is to use job evaluation systems that value jobs by a points system. This might entail measuring the relative complexity, training, and responsibility of female-dominated secretarial jobs and male-dominated construction jobs within a firm. Once the "value" of different jobs has been administratively assessed, an equitable wage scale can be applied. This scale may deviate substantially from market wage rates for the jobs in question. Any application of this technique raises three practical problems:

- Any administrative system of job evaluation is highly subjective. How can one be sure of the value of dirty manual labor (say, that of a cleaner in an abattoir) relative to the value of concentration and manual dexterity (say, that of a seamstress in a textile factory)? The former jobs may be dominated by men and the latter dominated by women, but any system that seeks to assign points to them objectively cannot avoid arbitrary decisions.

- Job evaluation systems require an expensive bureaucracy to do the valuations entailed. The per employee costs are unjustifiably high for all but the largest employers. Bilson talks about the "increasingly bureaucratic organization of the modern workplace" and wishes the reader to infer — wrongly — that such job evaluation systems could be easily put in place. On this score, I refer the reader to Betcherman's conclusion that nontraditional workplaces are gaining ground.

Firms using these nontraditional models typically cannot afford such systems, nor do the rigidities of job valuation systems fit with the "nontraditional" style.

- In practice, the demand for equal pay for work of equal value always becomes a demand for wage increases. The solution to pay "inequities" is to raise the pay of those suffering discrimination — in short, to raise the pay of women whose pay is systematically low relative to that of men in jobs of similar value. Surely, in principle, we should adjust all wages to a new "equitable" level partway between former levels. If women are being underpaid in relation to their value, men are being inequitably overpaid. To tackle pay equity through simultaneous increases and decreases in wages would refute the argument of employers that pay equity is simply a cost increase.

I do not deny the continued survival of some systemic inequities between men and women at work in Canada. But, in summary, pay equity systems are administratively costly, contain arbitrary elements, and are in effect complicated substitutes for collective bargaining or supply and demand as a means of negotiating wage increases. Bilson relies on old data to make a case about the severity of sexual discrimination. I suggest that continuing changes in the nature of work, together with the almost complete switch to two-earner families (with the man no longer the dominant wage earner) are doing what laws, regulations, and bureaucracy have failed, and will always fail, to accomplish. Suffice it to say, history is full of examples of judicial and legal interference on behalf of some collectivity that has gone radically wrong.

Having thrown cold water on many of the ideas of my fellow contributors to this book, I may rightly be asked, "What is your solution?" While this is not my assignment, I shall not dodge the question. Earlier, I mentioned the importance of industrial relations systems that correct themselves without undue damage to society. This is related to my preference for an economic system as close as feasible to a free market. Not that the solution generated by the market at any given time is necessarily ideal; it may well be inferior to a planned result. But unattractive market outcomes will correct themselves faster than unattractive outcomes arising from government rules and regulations. Consider three examples:

- Market economies admittedly generate bouts of high unemployment, and a generous unemployment insurance (UI) system that removes the poverty caused by job loss seems, on first consideration, an attractive political measure. Starting in 1971, Canada made its UI system particularly generous — diverging from US systems, which follow more closely the actuarial principles of insurance. A quarter-century later, most Canadians recognize the effect of perverse incentives that subsidize seasonal industries and long-term unemployment. But now, entire regions and industries lobby strenuously to preserve the inefficient status quo. Had Canadian UI remained closer to actuarial principles — with experience-rated premiums, no regional extended benefits to discourage mobility, and stronger links between work and benefits — Canadian unemployment rates would be closer to those in the United States.

- Betcherman is concerned about labor market rigidities associated with the segmenting of employment into standard and nonstandard jobs. He does not analyze the extent to which legislated labor standards are the cause. These standards generate costs, such as UI and Canada and Quebec Pension Plan premiums, that increase employer's wage costs above the wages paid. To minimize such payroll taxes, firms make greater use of part-time workers. Government labor standards have contributed significantly to the growth in nonstandard jobs that Betcherman laments.

- Labor codes that make union certification easy and decertification difficult are another source of Canada's high unemployment relative to that in the United States. Rather than compare our high level of strike activity to the artificially low European statistics, we should ask ourselves why our southern neighbor, in so many ways the most adversarial country in the world, has a more peaceful labor record. The answer lies in the fact that it is much easier for US workers to dislodge unions that foster policies inimical to workers' economic well-being. In the United States, strikes over ideological matters are less frequent. Also, because it is easier for firms to hire replacement workers, the cost of a prolonged strike in the United States is more likely to be the loss of the strikers' jobs. Workers and their unions think twice before embarking on a work stoppage. Unions are part of a necessary system of checks and balances between employer and employee, but in Canada the balance is very much in the unions' favor. Canadian unions are entrenched and can afford longer and more frequent work stoppages than US unions.

Nonetheless, we should try to develop institutions that foster better cooperation and understanding between unions and management. Many Canadian chief executive officers have never dealt with unions throughout their entire careers. Many labor leaders have little practical understanding of the painful choices required by those running a business in a competitive global economy. Some gulfs of misunderstanding have been bridged by bipartite union-management organizations such as the Canadian Steel Trade and Employment Congress (of which I am co-chairman), the Western Wood Products Forum, and the Sectoral Skills Council of the Electric and Electronics Industry. These organizations have required union officials and senior management to work on issues of mutual interest as opposed to the zero-sum issues that arise in collective bargaining.

Finally, I cannot resist a comment on the state of public education. Both Adams and Betcherman favor workplace training. While such training can be valuable, we cannot ignore a basic fact: Canada shares with the United States the deserved reputation of producing badly trained starting workers. We have allowed our public schools to evolve into a system in which graduation is based on seniority, not measurement of performance. Workplace training is no substitute for good schools.

References

The Economist. 1995. "Economic Indicators." July 15.

Organisation for Economic Co-operation and Development. 1995. *OECD Economic Outlook* 57 (June).

Swedish Institute. 1994. "The Swedish Economy." *Fact Sheets on Sweden*. Stockholm. November.

Comment:
Labor Markets and Deficits

John O'Grady

Two deficits define the context for social policy over the next decade. The first is the *fiscal deficit*; the second, the *social deficit*. The evidence of the past decade underscores that the two deficits are closely related. A deterioration in the fiscal deficit frustrates efforts to redress the social deficit. Conversely, a widening of the social deficit triggers program spending that hinders efforts to contain the fiscal deficit. It is a serious error, therefore, to cast the twin deficits as rival centerpieces for policy.

The social deficit arises from the inability of Canadians in the bottom 40 percent of the income scale to achieve a morally acceptable level of economic security from the labor market and from private arrangements to deal with illness, disability, and unemployment. Today, fiscal pressures clearly preclude any strategies to redress this deficit through increases in public spending. Indeed, the 1995 federal budget set Canada on the course of reducing social spending as a proportion of gross domestic product (GDP). If reductions in spending are the sole determinant of how social policy will be reformed, the pattern of the past ten years will be replicated. Reductions in social spending will lead directly to an increase in the social deficit, and the widening of the social deficit will lead to unanticipated increases in social spending. While the overall fiscal position may be alleviated in public sector finance, the net improvement will be substantially less than expected. A critical question, therefore, is whether there are interventions in the labor market and in human resource management practices that will improve the economic security of the bottom 40 percent of Canadians and thereby reduce the pressure for increased in social spending.

Opinion on the right typically advocates rolling back intervention by governments and unions in the labor market and in the determination of human resource management. The caption for these steps is "restoring flexibility and competitiveness." The social deficit, when it is considered explicitly, is seen as being alleviated through traditional, trickle-down economics and the removal of disincentives to work. The unemployment insurance (UI) system and social assistance, we are given to understand, are redolent with these disincentives. There is little that is new in any of this wine, save perhaps the bottle from which it is served. As Robbie Burns wrote, "Go fetch me a pint o'wine, An' fill it in a silver tassie."

Until the bracing experience of actually governing in major provinces in the 1990s, most of the Canadian left saw the fiscal deficit, if not as benign, at least as not a defining priority for economic policy. Spending on social programs was exonerated by pointing to higher social spending in other industrialized countries whose fiscal deficits were less aggravated. Opinion on the left favored, and continues to favor, some combination of tougher employment standards, expanded collective bargaining, and interventions in employers' practices in managing human resources. The past decade saw numerous innovations in administrative law, including legislation addressing pay and employment equity, the application of human rights codes to remedying systemic discrimination, and human resource guidelines for private sector suppliers of services to governments. Not surprisingly, the left has little sympathy for weakening the regulation of the labor market and broadening employers' discretion over human resource management practices. There is, however, disagreement — sometimes considerable disagreement — on the relative weights that should be attached to collective bargaining, employment standards, and, most recently, equity-oriented administrative law.

The Twin Deficits

To appreciate the link between the fiscal deficit and the social deficit, it is useful to review their dimensions and their causes. The fiscal deficit arises, of course, from the difference between revenues and expenditures in the public sector. In aggregate, that difference has been negative for Canadian governments in every year since 1975. In most jurisdictions, however, public sector revenues are sufficient — or close to sufficient — to cover *program* spending. The imbalance arises from the interest charges on the public sector's accumulated debt. Debt service charges are the proximate determinant of the size of the overall fiscal deficit and thus the increase in the amount of outstanding debt.

The real interest rate on this debt now exceeds the long-term growth potential of the Canadian economy. The arithmetic of the debt overhang is, therefore, inescapable. Without a reduction in program spending, an increase in taxes, or the sale of public sector assets, both the debt and the interest burden will increase. The growing claim of debt service on current revenues will mean that all levels of the public sector will experience reduced capacity to meet program commitments. *Ad hoc* controls on the wages of public employees may diminish, for a time, the severity of this pressure,[1] but they will not alter the fundamental arithmetic of the crisis in public sector finance.

---

[1] The public sector wage premium is a secondary source of fiscal pressure. In a recent study (O'Grady 1994), I compare negotiated wage increases in Ontario for the 1978–91 period. The cumulative increase for all industries was 41.5 percent. For local governments where the right to strike or lockout operates, the cumulative increase was 44.8 percent. In the health and welfare industries that are predominantly ruled by arbitration, the cumulative increase was 49.7 percent. Wages negotiated by the provincial government, also subject to arbitration, rose 47.8 percent. If public sector wage increases had been on par with the all-industries average, the 1991 public sector wage bill in Ontario would have been 3.3 to 8.4 percent less (depending on the subsector).

The province's 1993 "social contract" removed $2 billion from public sector budgets, whose aggregate payroll was roughly $43 million. The reduction was largely, though not entirely, borne by public sector payrolls; overall public sector compensation fell by approximately 4.5 percent.

In extremis, the limit on a fiscal deficit is reached when an actual or a feared default makes private financing unavailable for new public sector debt issues. For the federal government, the financing limit would be reflected in foreign lenders' deciding to reduce their holdings of Canadian government debt. Roughly one-quarter of the federal government's debt is held by non-residents; the average term to maturity of the debt is less than five years; and more than half the outstanding instruments mature in less than three years, the Bank of Canada tells us. The high proportion of nonresident holdings and the debt's term structure make us acutely vulnerable to swings in international lenders' confidence. The currency crisis that would unfold in the wake of a loss of that confidence would force drastic fiscal actions on the federal government.

For the provincial governments, hitting the financing limit would lead to negotiating the terms of borrowing support with the federal government or perhaps the Bank of Canada as the federal government's agent.

Less dramatic but no less real than the danger of "hitting the debt wall" is the effect of the debt overhang on real interest rates. High debt service costs inevitably aggravate fears that the debt will be monetized and that the consequent inflation will erode the value of long-term bonds. As a result, the risk premium built into long-term interest rates has spiked. Real interest rates, both long term and short term, are now at levels that radically constrain the economy's achievable growth rates. The weakness of the domestic economy's response to the current export-led recovery is largely explained by the effects of high real interest rates. Higher unemployment — especially long-term unemployment — is an inevitable consequence. It now seems likely that Canada will enter the next cyclical slowdown with unemployment of more than 8 percent. Inexorably, the failure to address the fiscal deficit will lead to an increase in the social deficit.

The social deficit is fundamentally about the distribution of income and economic security. The labor market and private insurance do not provide the bottom two-fifths of Canadians with an acceptable degree of protection against the economic effects of illness, disability, or unemployment. It was to address this social deficit that Canadians put in place the welfare state, which lies at the heart of the current debate over public sector finance.

The welfare state structure rests on three pillars. The first is the system of transfer payments to individuals, for which there are no dedicated taxes; Old Age Security (OAS) payments, the Guaranteed Income Supplement (GIS), and the Canada Assistance Plan (CAP) are the most important. The second is the social insurance system, of which the major pieces are UI and the Canada and Quebec Pension Plans (CPP/QPP), along with workers' compensation at the provincial level; in principle, they are financed by dedicated payroll taxes. The third pillar is governments' direct spending on social services; health care and education account for the preponderance of this spending.

Since the radical expansion of UI coverage in 1971, the design of welfare state benefits has moved in opposite directions. Successive changes to the system restricted access to UI benefits. On the other hand, social assistance benefits — after lagging changes in average wages — were improved in many jurisdictions, as were workers' compensation benefits. Some provinces enriched their supplements to the federal GIS; at the same time, OAS benefits were subjected to an income-tested clawback tax. On balance, it can be argued that changes in the design of social programs have balanced each other, yielding fiscal neutrality since 1971. Thus, changes in overall spending by the welfare state have been determined chiefly by demographic factors, the degree of slack in the labor market, and payroll pressure on directly delivered services.

Figure 1 tracks the increase in public sector spending over time, and Figure 2 compares changes in spending on programs (that is, spending net of interest charges) with changes in the level of unemployment. Public spending as a percentage of GDP ratchets up when there is a deterioration in the labor market and

Figure 1:   *Public Sector Spending*
**   *as a Percentage of GDP, 1950–93***

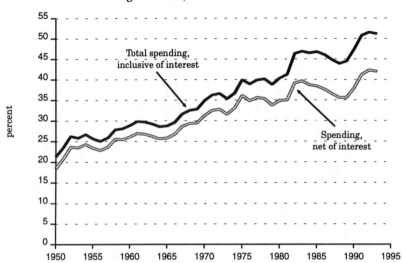

Note: Spending data are on a National Accounts basis for the aggregate public sector
       (federal, provincial, and municipal).
Source: Canada 1994.

falls off when conditions improve. On a cyclical basis, an increase
in the social deficit causes an increase in the fiscal deficit. Policymakers have long recognized this relationship. What is less
noted is that the long-term increase in public sector spending is
also rooted in a long-term increase in the social deficit.

Gordon Betcherman's contribution to this volume reviews
the evidence that points incontestably to an increase in the social
deficit over the past two decades. Unemployment increased from
an average of 6.7 percent in the 1970s to 9.3 percent in the 1980s.
The prospect for the 1990s is for little improvement; indeed, over
the first five years of this decade, unemployment has averaged
10.3 percent. Behind this upward trend is a still more disturbing
increase in the incidence of long-term unemployment, which
especially affects blue-collar workers who lose their jobs as a
result of trade- or technology-related restructuring. Accentuating
polarization has been an increase in the proportion of jobs that

Figure 2: *Public Sector Spending and Unemployment, Year-over-Year Changes, 1968–93*

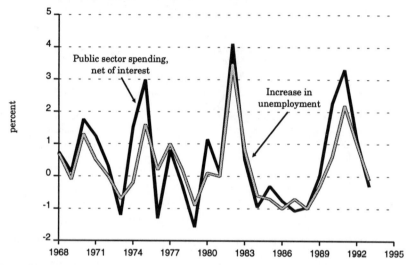

Note: Spending data are on a National Accounts basis for the aggregate public sector (federal, provincial, and municipal).

Source: Canada 1994.

are characterized by poor wages, few benefits, short tenure, and negligible employers' investment in training. What Betcherman — and before him, the Economic Council of Canada — terms "nonstandard employment"[2] increased from less than 24 percent of total employment in the mid-1970s to almost 30 percent in 1993. For many classes of workers, earnings dispersion widened. For male workers, Betcherman reports that "real, annual earnings for the bottom quintile (fifth) decreased by 16.3 percent between 1973 and 1989 while, at the same time, they increased

---

2 "Nonstandard employment" embraces all employment-like relationships other than full-time, permanent employment. Since "employment" may be described as permanent when it is not limited to a specific period of time, nonstandard employment includes part-time work, short-term or contract work, assignments that are channeled through employment agencies, and self-employment. Belous (1989) uses the term "contingent work." The International Labour Office (Rodgers and Janine 1989) uses "precarious employment" and "atypical employment."

by 7.9 percent for the upper quintile." The analysis that Betcherman presents confirms the earlier finding of the Economic Council of Canada (1990) that there is "a growing segmentation in the labour market...[and] that the labour market is offering economic security to fewer Canadians" (p. 17).

The increase in the social deficit that Betcherman describes has been an important driver behind the growth in the fiscal deficit. The deterioration in the labor market is experienced disproportionately by the bottom 40 percent of Canadians. It is they who are most at risk of losing their jobs. It is also they who are most vulnerable to long spells of unemployment and to re-employment in jobs that offer low wages, few benefits, and little security. Nonstandard employment is confined mainly to the bottom 40 percent of the labor force and is most frequent in the bottom quintile. As Betcherman and others note, it is these Canadians who have been on the losing end of the increasing dispersion in incomes.

The increase in the social deficit puts pressure on the welfare state to make good at least some of the loss in economic security. The widening social deficit leads to more and longer UI claims, swelling social assistance rolls, increased use of the CPP through early retirement benefits, and greater need for GISs. Though the relationship is more complex and less certain, there also appears to be a link between the increase in the social deficit and greater use of both the health care system and workers' compensation (Evans 1994).

The shock to public sector finance can be traced to the recession of the early 1980s. Unemployment jumped from 7.5 percent in 1981 to 11.0 percent in 1982 and 11.8 percent in 1983, subsiding only to 11.2 percent in 1984 and 10.5 percent in 1985. At the same time, the deficit for the public sector jumped from $5.2 billion (1.5 percent of GDP) in 1981 to $22.2 billion in 1982.[3]

---

3 The deficit, spending, and revenue figures given here are current dollar amounts for the aggregate Canadian public sector (federal, provincial, and municipal) measured on a National Accounts basis.

By 1985, it reached $32.5 billion (6.8 percent of GDP). From 1981
to 1985, public sector revenues actually rose from $141.6 billion
to $191.0 billion, but public sector spending (net of interest
charges) increased more quickly, from $124.6 billion to $183.3 billion (Canada 1994).

The lingering effects of that recession prevented spending
on social programs from returning to prerecession averages. High
spending coupled with a spike in interest rates and the increase
in accumulated debt seriously imbalanced the fiscal position of
the public sector. During the latter half of the 1980s, that imbalance eased, but it deteriorated sharply during the recession of the
early 1990s. By 1993, even excluding interest charges, public
sector spending as a proportion of GDP stood at more than
42 percent — higher than at any time since World War II and its
immediate aftermath.

Breaking the Cycle

The twin deficits reinforce and exacerbate each other. An increase
in the incidence of economic insecurity puts pressure on income
replacement and augmentation systems, and when spending
increases to meet the demands generated by a rising social deficit,
the fiscal imbalance deteriorates. Debt service charges ratchet
up, claiming an ever higher proportion of current revenues.
Inevitably, the consequence is impairment of the public sector's
ability to meet its program commitments.

One option — favored by conservative opinion — is to mar-
shall the political will to roll back spending and accept the adverse
consequences of economic insecurity and maldistribution of economic opportunity. A second course, which the papers in this
volume explore, starts by looking at the institutions and rules
that shape labor market outcomes. Comparative analysis undertaken in the United States by the National Bureau of Economic
Research underscores the fact that differences in institutions and
regulatory regimes can result in markedly different labor market

results (Freeman 1994). In a similar vein, the International Labour Office shows that labor standards condition the way that adjustment occurs at the firm level (Sengenberger and Campbell 1994; Standing and Tokman 1991).

At issue is the relationship between labor market institutions and the social deficit. The contributors to this volume hold that some types of labor market regulation bring about a more equitable distribution of economic security and also encourage productivity-enhancing investment. The implication is that there are two routes, not just one, to reducing the social deficit. The first is the *social policy route*, which requires increasing amounts of direct spending by governments to offset the inequitable distribution of economic security. The second is the *labor market route*, which relies on changing the workings of the labor market to achieve the same objective. The latter holds out the possibility of governments' reducing program spending to restore fiscal balance while they rely on changes to labor market institutions to prevent the social deficit from deteriorating. This strategy is the essence of the social democratic approach to the two deficits.

The relationship between the social deficit and labor market regulation can be framed in terms of four questions.

- Are firms encouraged to externalize or internalize the cost of adjusting to changes in market circumstances? Firms externalize adjustment costs when they achieve flexibility by turning to nonstandard forms of employment, which place the cost of adjustment on individuals, reducing their economic security and thus increasing demands on the social security system. When the incidence of nonstandard employment is increasing — as it is now — these effects are significant.

- Does labor market regulation encourage firms to invest in developing their employees' skills? Clearly, firms will not invest to any significant degree in employees who are temporary or part time. Even within the framework of full-time, permanent employment relationships, some types of work organization are more conducive than others to investment in human resource development. Yet firms' failure to invest in that development raises adjustment costs when structural changes compel workers to seek new employment. These adjustment costs have recently been evident in the sharp rise in the incidence of long-term unemployment, especially among blue-collar workers.

- Does labor market regulation reduce the dispersion of earnings? The Organisation for Economic Co-operation and Development (OECD 1993) finds that earnings inequality increased in 12 of 17 countries during the 1980s, and it cites institutional factors — the various systems of organization, legislation, and custom that govern the way workers are employed and deployed — as an important cause of the differing patterns. Edin and Zetterberg (1992) also stress the role of labor market institutions, noting that "the variability of wages across industries is about three times as large in the United States as it is in Sweden" (p. 1342). Kreuger and Summers (1987) report that the standard deviation (coefficient of variation) of manufacturing sector wages in the United States and in Canada is approximately equal (0.241 and 0.239, respectively) but substantially larger than that in Sweden (0.081), France (0.126), Germany (0.141), or the United Kingdom (0.140). At the enterprise level, Freeman (1982) finds that unionized establishments have a marked tendency to apply single wage rates to an occupation or to use an automatic progression whereas nonunion establishments are more likely to determine wages on the basis of individual performance. Greater earnings inequality and greater wage dispersion are the other side of the coin of the increase in economic insecurity that took place in the 1980s. Although there is no consistent relationship between earnings inequality and demands on a social security system, a political system is likely to translate an increase in economic insecurity into pressures on the income redistribution and income support systems.

- What impact does labor market regulation have on overall employment growth? In the 1980s, it was commonplace to contrast job creation in the United States with the much poorer record in Europe. The implication was the existence of a tradeoff between job creation and employment protection. At the same time, commentators were puzzled by the widespread — and apparently voluntary — practice of Japanese companies in providing a degree of employment security without parallel elsewhere in the OECD. The Japanese experience suggests that a simple tradeoff model may fail to capture the role of employment security in motivating workers and generating compensating productivity gains. *The OECD Jobs Study* suggests that employment protection legislation in Germany led to "a virtuous circle of employment stability, training and low unemployment" (1994, 80). The minimum wage — that other bugaboo of conservatives — is also being considered in a new light following recent empirical work in the United States (Card and Kreuger 1995).

The contributions to this volume stress the importance of institutional factors in labor market outcomes and, by inference, in the incidence of economic insecurity. Betcherman examines the role of human resource management practices in externalizing or internalizing adjustment costs, pointing out that the UI system provides employers with powerful incentives to rely on layoffs and thereby to externalize adjustment costs. Adams considers the contribution that cooperative industrial relations systems, especially works councils and centralized bargaining, make to overall economic performance, arguing that cooperative industrial relations systems have a demonstrable impact on productivity and on the management of adjustment processes. Although he does not make the claim, the reader may infer that, by internalizing adjustment costs and encouraging more rapid innovation, cooperative industrial relations systems reduce the demands placed on the social security system. (The evidence on this point, as I discuss later, is mixed.) Bilson reviews the role of rights-based regulation that uses administrative boards vested with remedial authority to enforce pay and employment equity as well as broad applications of equity standards under human rights codes.

Not specifically addressed by the contributors to this volume is the degree to which various types of labor market interventions re-enforce, or substitute for one another. Would expanding the coverage of collective bargaining accelerate the trend toward human resource management models that internalize adjustment costs? What is the relationship between collective bargaining and rights-based regulation through tribunals? Finally, to what degree is it realistic to envision an evolution of our decentralized, adversarial industrial relations system to a more cooperative, centralized structure?

Models of Human Resources Management

Betcherman bases his analysis on the findings of the Human Resource Practices Survey (HRPS) that he and his colleagues carried out for *The Canadian Workplace in Transition* report (Betcherman 1994). He distinguishes three models of human resource management. The first, which he characterizes as *traditional*, is based on narrow job definitions, limited employee participation in decisionmaking, straight compensation systems (without incentive features), and little employer investment in training. This model is widespread in the manufacturing and resource industries, where collective bargaining has superimposed seniority rules, litigious job evaluation, and a style of unionism that emphasizes strict enforcement of job demarcation lines as a strategy to preserve employment. The HRPS conservatively estimates that 53 percent of Canadian workplaces conformed to the main features of the traditional model in 1993.

(Given the survey's bias toward larger establishments, Betcherman believes its results underestimate the prevalence of this model.)

An important consequence of the traditional model is that it achieves flexibility by externalizing the costs of adjustment. Both short-term and permanent layoffs are recurrent features. So also is reliance on part-time or contingent workers. Richard Belous (1989) of the National Planning Association in Washington, DC, argues that the drive to achieve flexibility *within* the terms of the traditional model has led many US companies to increase their use of part-time and casual workers or workers supplied by temporary-service agencies. Estimating the proportion of these "contingent" workers in the United States, he concludes that their share of the employed labor force increased from a range of 25.0 to 28.5 percent in 1980 to 29.9 to 36.6 percent by 1988. Betcherman reaches comparable conclusions on both the magnitude of the change in nonstandard work and the origins of the change in human resource management.

Job definitions are comparatively narrow in workplaces that adhere to the traditional model.[4] When a job cycle (the time required to complete a process) is as short as one minute, little training is required. If employees in these firms subsequently lose their jobs, they are often ill-equipped to secure new employment that offers good wages and better tenure — jobs that typically require a higher entry level of human capital and are offered to inside candidates before outsiders are considered.

The consequences of externalized adjustment costs are significant, both for workers and for the demands that are placed on welfare state programs. This conclusion is confirmed by a Statistics Canada longitudinal study (Picot and Wannel 1987) of the roughly 1 million workers who lost their jobs between 1981 and 1984. By 1986, only 31 to 35 percent of them had found re-

---

4 By way of contrast, Osterman (1988, 124ff) compares the number of job classifications in a US auto assembly plant and a Swedish plant. The former may have a hundred different job classifications. In the Swedish plant, workers are effectively grouped in six job grades.

employment on a full-time basis with a wage loss of no more than 10 percent. An estimated 26 percent of those who were re-employed had suffered a real wage loss, which averaged 28 percent. It is hardly surprising, in these circumstances, that the demands on welfare state programs increased during the recession of the 1980s and remained high thereafter.[5]

Betcherman contrasts both compensation-based and participation-based models of human resource management with the traditional model. The former relies on sophisticated compensation systems and variable pay to induce employees to greater commitment and flexibility. The participation-based model puts more emphasis on team methods of production. Both systems organize work around broader job definitions than the traditional models, and employer investment in training is substantially higher. The reliance on layoffs is markedly lower — a pattern consistent with higher rates of investment in training. Betcherman estimates that the compensation-based and the participation-based models have approximately equal prevalence; they accounted for 23 and 24 percent, respectively, of the sample in the HRPS.

Firms that have adopted compensation-based or participation-based models achieve operational flexibility through cooperation, commitment, and broadly trained employees. For these firms, layoffs entail a real loss of human capital and organizational capacity. As a result, they rely much less on layoffs, preferring to use attrition or worksharing to deal with reduced labor needs. Moreover, those firms frequently give workers who are laid off considerable assistance in obtaining re-employment. The investment they have made in their employees' skills facilitates re-employment in jobs that offer approximately comparable tenure and wages. It can be argued, then, that compensation-based and participation-based models both internalize adjustment costs to a greater degree than the traditional model and increase the

---

5 An extensive economic literature describes the hysteresis (lingering) effects of a deep recession. See, for example, Blanchard and Summers (1991).

proportion of "good" jobs. Certainly, if the growth of nonstandard or contingent employment could be arrested, let alone reversed, the implications for the social deficit would be significant; there would be more scope to address the fiscal deficit and restore public sector finances to a maintainable balance.

What is not clear, however, is whether the shift toward compensation-based and participation-based models reduces or merely masks the bifurcation of workers into "core" and "periphery" employees. By increasing their reliance on outsourcing and subcontracting, companies that appear to be internalizing adjustment costs may be divesting themselves of those costs through other means. When market conditions become more competitive, firms seek to reduce fixed costs, including those associated with employees. Costs that can be avoided will be avoided.

Collective Bargaining and Pay Equity

If the impact of a shift in models of human resource management is uncertain, there is more consensus about the effects of collective bargaining. Comparative studies indicate that an unvarying characteristic of collective bargaining is its strong bias toward standardizing wages and benefits across firms within a sector. This is understandable. Taking wages out of competition is fundamental to union strategy, and accomplishing that goal requires either formal, multi-employer bargaining or, more commonly in North America, pattern bargaining. Regardless of the formal bargaining structure used, the effect is the same: reduction of wage dispersion among employees in comparable occupations and compression of the wage hierarchy. Unions also seek, with varying degrees of success, to curtail the use of part-time labor and contracting out. When part-time employees are covered by collective agreements, there is a noticeable tendency to extend fringe benefits, at least on a prorated basis.

Patricia McDermott (1991) finds, in a study for the Ontario Ministry of Labour, that multi-employer bargaining and high rates of collective bargaining coverage demonstrably narrow the male-female wage gap. This finding is important to keep in mind when appraising the capacity of collective bargaining to address equity issues. Beth Bilson, in her contribution to this volume, states the case for intervention in the operation of labor markets by tribunals mandated to apply equity standards. Ontario's pay equity and employment equity tribunals are examples of this model. So also are the increasingly activist human rights commissions in most jurisdictions. (The annual reports of the Ontario Human Rights Commission consistently show that more than 70 percent of complaints it receives arise from employment situations.)

Bilson's attraction to rights-based litigation and activist tribunals arises from her reservations about the operation of collective bargaining. Though supportive of collective bargaining, Bilson sympathizes with the "advocates of equity programs...[who] have been reluctant to entrust unions with exclusive responsibility for the pursuit of equality for workers." Unions, she notes,

> have not themselves been perfectly free of discriminatory practices and assumptions. The white male workers who have had the predominant influence in union leadership and the formulation of collective bargaining positions in large part share their employers' assumptions about appropriate ranking of jobs, the needs of male and female workers' and the status of part-time workers.

The inference is that white-male-dominated unions, left to their own devices, are more likely to ratify inequalities than they are to correct them. Proactive pay equity and employment equity legislation, enforced by mandated tribunals, is necessary to alter the conservative wage and opportunity structure that unions would otherwise maintain or, at least, fail to challenge.

A common objection to rights-based adjudication by tribunals is that the operation of the labor market tends, by its own logic, to extinguish discriminatory practices. Discrimination involves paying a certain class of people a wage that is less than the marginal value they create. This situation is not a sustainable equilibrium, the argument runs, so other firms will identify the opportunity to offer a somewhat higher wage and still benefit from a marginal product that exceeds the wage; over time, the gap between actual wages and marginal product will be closed.

This view offers numerous difficulties. First, an economy, such as ours, that is characterized by a large overhang on the labor market provides ample scope for the persistence of discriminatory practices. Second, because information on prospective employees is costly to obtain, employers frequently rely on "signals" to appraise candidates. These signals may be relatively benign, such as years of education or prior work experience, but they may be race and gender. Finally, there is an important link between the internal labor markets that Betcherman examines and the persistence of inequitable wage structures. Many firms — especially larger firms — pay above-market wages, which, Bilson notes, significantly insulate human resource decisions from the direct pressure of market forces.

Gunderson and Riddell (1991) summarize empirical research on gender-based wage differentials. They conclude that, after controlling for productivity-related factors and adjusting for differences in average hours, "an earnings gap remains that is difficult to account for other than as reflecting discrimination" (p. 159). Ontario (1985) estimates the magnitude of this gap in the mid-1980s at 15 to 20 percent.[6] Significantly, the analysts find that the earnings gap tends to be smaller when comparisons are made within the same establishment rather than across establishments. Gunderson and Riddell (1991) conclude that this phenomenon reflects the tendency of women to be disproportionately

---

6 The econometric analysis presented in the green paper finds an unadjusted ratio of female-male wages for full-year, full-time employees of 0.62, signaling a wage gap of 0.38, which is decomposed as follows: 0.16 attributable to differences in hours worked, 0.05 to 0.10 to experience, education, and unionization, 0.10 to 0.15 to occupational segregation, and 0.05 to wage discrimination.

employed in lower-wage establishments. An important implication of this finding is that pay equity legislation that is focused on within-establishment or within-firm comparisons will have a comparatively modest impact on remedying the wage gap. More substantive progress would be made by expanding the scope for multi-employer bargaining.

To underscore the importance of broader-based, (multi-employer) bargaining is not to dismiss the importance of pay equity legislation. As Bilson points out, such legislation establishes important normative principles that influence the behavior of private parties. Nevertheless, introducing elaborate rights-based legislation while leaving intact a highly fragmented, decentralized structure of collective bargaining is rather like putting the chassis of a Cadillac on a scooter. One should not be surprised if the result disappoints.

Some readers probably share Bilson's reservations about collective bargaining and endorse her emphasis on rights-based, litigious processes. Others, however, may feel that broader-based bargaining, albeit with the normative direction of pay equity standards, offers a more efficacious route. This may especially be the case in the private sector, where resources for litigation are limited and additional money to finance equity adjustments is less forthcoming.

Without an organized voice, it is difficult to see how rights-based processes can be expected to have any pervasive effect on labor markets or on practices in human resource management. Ontario's *Occupational Health and Safety Act,* for example, confers the same right to refuse unsafe work on union and nonunion employees alike. The number of occasions when nonunion employees have exercised this right is close to zero. It seems unlikely that this phenomenon indicates that nonunion employers provide safer workplaces. A more likely explanation is that rights conferred on individual workers are of little practical consequence when those workers do not enjoy representation by an independent union or an autonomous works council.

Some commentators view union constraints on managerial discretion with the same disfavor that they view the tribunal-based interventions that Bilson defends. Canada, they point out, is not Germany. Union strategy in Canada — as in other Anglo-American jurisdictions — tends toward what has been called "job-control unionism,"[7] a tradition that conflicts with many aspects of the compensation-based and participation-based models of human resource management that Betcherman describes. The conflict is not insurmountable. Indeed, many unionized workplaces have introduced participation-based models. There is also some evidence that participation-based innovations have greater durability in unionized plants (Mishel and Voos 1991). Nevertheless, the bias of job-control unionism is to replicate and articulate what Betcherman terms a traditional model of human resource management.

Industrial Relations

Although collective bargaining applies to only a minority of workers in the private sector, it would be a serious error to underestimate its relevance to the functioning of the labor market and to practices in human resource management. Approximately 60 percent of nonoffice employees in the manufacturing and resource industries are covered by collective agreements.[8] It is

---

7 The term "job-control unionism" was introduced into industrial relations literature in the 1980s. The earliest and most extensive discussion is Piore (1982). The concept is further elaborated in Piore and Sabel (1984, ch. 5). Other discussions are Katz (1987) and Kochan, Katz, and McKersie (1986). Thelen (1991) contrasts North American job-control unionism with union strategy in West Germany, and O'Grady (forthcoming) discusses its nature in some detail.

8 It is important to distinguish between union membership as a percentage of employed workers and collective agreement coverage. The latter tends to be greater. One should also distinguish between a sector's total workforce and its nonoffice workforce. Collective agreement coverage is largely confined to the latter group, which is approximately 70 percent of the workforce in...

simply not possible, in these industries, to address issues of
human resource management without taking account of industrial relations factors.

In this volume, Roy Adams summarizes the evidence that
cooperative industrial relations have pervasive effects on an
economy. The benefits flow principally through two channels. The
first operates at the level of the workplace. Cooperative industrial
relations increase a firm's capacity to innovate and adapt and also
the productivity gains that arise from learning-by-doing. (Lazonick
[1990, appendix] describes the beneficial interaction among investment, innovation and cooperative shop floor relations.)

The second channel through which cooperative industrial
relations potentially benefit an economy operates at the macroeconomic level. A cooperative system of industrial relations, the
argument runs, permits a more favorable tradeoff between inflation and unemployment, which increases the potential growth
rate of the economy. Cooperative industrial relations systems
tend to be more centralized — that is, bargaining takes place on
a multi-employer basis. This stands to reason. Centralization
makes the macroeconomic consequences of union strategy ger-
mane to the conduct of bargaining. Centralization may also
enable the negotiation of framework agreements within which
innovation at the workplace can proceed with union support. This
situation appears to have been significant in Sweden and Australia, though not in Germany or Japan.

In the 1970s and 1980s, the evidence supported the claim of
a relationship between centralized bargaining and a more advan-
tageous tradeoff between inflation and unemployment. The record for the past five years is less convincing. Northern Europe,
with its centralized collective bargaining systems, has weathered

---

Note 8 - cont'd.

   ...manufacturing and resource industries. (Collective agreement coverage by
   sector is reported in Statistics Canada's 1990 Labour Market Activity Survey.
   For a summary and discussion of these survey results, see Riddell, 113–114.)

the current recession no better than North America, with its fragmented and adversarial system. Moreover, on both sides of the Atlantic, monetary policy — not wage policy — has been the principal instrument for containing inflation.

There is also reason to believe that the adjustment pressures that stem from globalization are posing difficulties for centralized bargaining systems. The Swedish system, in particular, has come under severe strain; how it will evolve is far from clear. What is clear, however, is that globalization is straining centralized bargaining structures. In North America, even pattern bargaining is yielding to the same pressures.

At the level of the individual firm, the impact of globalization is more differentiated. Two adjustment patterns are evident. Companies that rely on Betcherman's traditional human resource management pursue labor-cost-reduction strategies that are consistent with the logic of that model. Production is relocated to regions where wages are lower. The use of subcontractors and outsourcing increases. To reduce the quasi-fixed cost associated with permanent, full-time workers, more workers are hired on a part-time or short-term basis. This response to competitive pressure can be called *type one adjustment*. In contrast is *type two adjustment*: the diffusion of Betcherman's compensation-based and participation-based models. The increase in the incidence of the two latter models is directly attributable to the competitive pressures associated with globalization. Whether firms become type one or type two adjusters determines both the type of jobs they offer and the allocation of adjustment costs. When the type one adjustment predominates, the social deficit tends to increase. When the type two pattern predominates, the social deficit may be held in check (though insecurity may be shifted to the employees of subcontractors; to some degree, this is what occurs in Japan).

The way in which firms adjust to competitive pressures is shaped by a complex interaction of economic, social, and institutional factors. Among the important institutional factors are the rules that apply to labor adjustment and workplace governance. Campbell and Sengenberger (1994, 422) comment:

> the economic opportunities provided by [labor] standards are most significant in situations of industrial decline and harsh competition. In fact, it is in such situations that labor standards can make their strongest contribution because they prevent a relapse into parochial and short-term behaviour.

The United States represents the clearest case of an economy with a low level of articulation of standards on adjustment and workplace governance. The countries of western Europe, especially Germany, are at the opposite end of the spectrum. Indeed, the European trend appears to be toward further articulation of legislated standards respecting workplace governance. Recent European Union directives, for example, require large companies (those that operate throughout the EU market) to establish works councils on the German model. The holdout against this trend is the United Kingdom, but even there, a change in government will likely see the end of the British opt-out negotiated at Maastricht. Such a shift would represent an important weakening of the Anglo-American tradition in labor-management relations, which has viewed the rights of management as an extension of the rights of property (see Bok 1991). Because its presumption of management's rights is stronger than in other legal traditions, the Anglo-American tradition has been more adversarial, more oriented to job-control unionism, and more inclined to litigiousness, and government intervention has focused more on minimum standards rather than on mandated consultation.

Institutional arrangements from one country cannot be transplanted readily into another country. This is not to say, however, that a system of industrial relations is impervious to change. Australia is the clearest case of an Anglo-American jurisdiction that has transformed its industrial relations system in response to the pressure of globalization (see Mathews 1994).

Workplace restructuring in Australia is strongly influenced by accords between the Australian Council of Trade Unions and the Labour government.[9] Since the introduction of the first accord in 1983, the Australian system of industrial relations — once among the most adversarial — has been altered in fundamental ways. Successive accords have committed the unions to active cooperation with far-reaching changes in the design of jobs and occupational standards, the system of remuneration, the management of training, and the organization of work. In Betcherman's terms, what is being undertaken is a managed shift from a traditional to a participation-based mode of human resource management.

Conclusion

Though this volume is not framed as a debate, the contributions to it approach the question of the labor market and the social deficit quite differently. Bilson would advance the equity agenda through rights-based tribunals and mandated equity plans. Betcherman argues that, in conditions of rapid adjustment, the traditional model of human resources management exacerbates the social deficit by accentuating the polarization of the labor market; for him, a key question is how to foster the adoption of participation-based or compensation-based models that internalize the costs of adjustment to the firm. Adams stresses the role of industrial relations factors and the need for institutional arrangements that foster more cooperative relations between labor and management; by inference, he argues that the participation-

---

9 Although usually described as a form of social contract between the Australian government and the Australian labor movement, the accords have actually been agreements between the Australian Labour Party and the Australian Council of Trade Unions. (Most Australian unions are affiliated with the Labour Party.) The first accord, which was essentially an agreement on wage restraint in exchange for social program and tax reforms, was negotiated while that party was in opposition. See Hancock and Isaac (1992); and Ryloh (1994).

based model cannot predominate without societal institutions that move labor and management in that direction.

All three authors believe that institutions, policies, and labor standards matter. The rules of the game affect not only how the game is played but also the score.

References

Belous, Richard. 1989. *The Contingent Economy: The Growth of the Temporary, Part-time and Subcontracted Workforce*. Washington, DC: National Planning Association.

Betcherman, Gordon, et al. 1994. *The Canadian Workplace in Transition*. Kingston, Ont.: Queen's University IRC Press.

Blanchard, Olivier J., and Lawrence H. Summers. 1991. "Hysteresis in Unemployment." In N. Gregory Mankiw and David Romer, eds., *New Keynesian Economics*, vol 1. Cambridge, Mass.: MIT Press.

Bok, Derek C. 1971. "Reflections on the Distinctive Character of American Labor Laws." *Harvard Law Review* 84 (April).

Campbell, Duncan, and Werner Sengenberger. 1994. "Labour Standards, Economic Efficiency, and Development." In Werner Sengenberger and Duncan Campbell, eds., *Creating Economic Opportunities: The Role of Labour Standards in Industrial Restructuring*. Geneva: International Labour Office.

Canada. 1994. Department of Finance. *Economic and Fiscal Reference Tables*. Ottawa. September.

Card, David, and Alan B. Kreuger. 1995. *Myth and Measurement: The New Economics of the Minimum Wage*. Princeton, NJ: Princeton University Press.

Economic Council of Canada. 1990. *Good Jobs, Bad Jobs*. Ottawa: Supply and Services Canada.

Eden, Per-Anders, and Johnny Zetterberg. 1992. "Interindustry Wage Differentials: Evidence from Sweden and a Comparison with the United States." *American Economic Review* 82 (December).

Evans, Robert G., et al., eds. 1994. *Why Are Some People Healthy and Others Not? The Determinants of Health of Populations*. New York: Aldine de Gruyter.

Freeman, Richard B. 1982. "Union Wage Practices and Wage Dispersion with Establishments." *Industrial and Labor Relations Review* 36 (October).

—————. ed. 1994. *Working under Different Rules.* A National Bureau of Economic Research Project Report. New York: Russell Sage Foundation.

Gunderson, Morley, and W. Craig Riddell. 1991. "Economics of Women's Wages in Canada." *International Review of Comparative Public Policy* 3.

Hancock, Keith, and J.E. Isaac. 1992. "Australian Experiments in Wage Policy." *British Journal of Industrial Relations* 30 (June).

Katz, Harry. 1987. *Shifting Gears,* Cambridge, Mass.: MIT Press.

Kochan, Thomas, Harry Katz, and Robert McKersie. 1986. *The Transformation of American Industrial Relations.* New York: Basic Books.

Kreuger, Alan B., and Lawrence H. Summers. 1987. "Reflections on the Inter-Industry Wage Structure." In K. Lang and J.S. Leonard, eds., *Unemployment and the Structure of Labour Markets.* Oxford: Blackwell.

Lazonick, William. 1990. *Competitive Advantage on the Shop Floor.* Cambridge, Mass.: Harvard University Press.

Mathews, John. 1994. *Catching the Wage: Workplace Reform in Australia.* Ithaca, NY: ILR Press / Cornell University.

McDermott, Patricia. 1991. "Broader Based Bargaining and Closing the Wage Gap." Paper prepared for the Ontario Ministry of Labour. February. Photocopied.

Mishel, Lawrence, and Paula B. Voos. 1991. *Unions and Economic Competitiveness.* Armonk, NY: Economic Policy Institute/ M.E. Sharpe.

OECD. 1993. *Employment Outlook.* Paris: Organisation for Economic Co-operation and Development.

—————. 1994. *The OECD Jobs Study: Facts, Analysis, Strategies.* Paris: Organisation for Economic Co-operation and Development.

O'Grady, John A. 1994. *Arbitration and Its Ills.* Government and Competitiveness Project 94-05. Kingston, Ont.: Queen's University, School of Policy Studies.

—————. Forthcoming. *Job Control Unionism vs the New Human Resource Management Model.* Kingston, Ont.: Queen's University IRC Press.

Ontario. 1985. *Green Paper on Pay Equity*. Toronto: Attorney General's Office.

Osterman, Paul. 1988. *Employment Futures: Reorganization, Dislocation, and Public Policy*. New York: Oxford University Press.

Picot, Garnett, and Ted Wannell. 1987. *Job Loss and Labour Market Adjustment in the Canadian Economy*. Statistics Canada Research Paper Series, study no. 5. Ottawa.

Piore, Michael. 1982. "American Labor and the Industrial Crisis." *Challenge* 25 (March-April): reprinted in *Challenge,* anniversary issue (1987).

——, and Charles F. Sabel. 1984. *The Second Industrial Divide: Possibilities for Prosperity*. New York: Basic Books.

Riddell, W. Cragg. 1993. "Unionization in Canada and the United States." In David Card and Richard B. Freeman, eds., *Small Differences That Matter: Labor Markets and Income Maintenance in Canada and the United States*. Chicago: National Bureau of Economic Research/University of Chicago Press.

Rodgers, Gerry, and Janine Rodgers, eds. 1989. *Precarious Jobs in Labour Market Regulation: The Growth of Atypical Employment in Western Europe*. Geneva: International Institute for Labour Studies/ International Labour Office.

Sengenberger, Werner, and Duncan Campbell, eds. 1994. *Creating Economic Opportunities: The Role of Labour Standards in Industrial Restructuring*. Geneva: International Labour Office.

Standing, Guy, and Victor Tokman, eds. 1991. *Towards Social Adjustment: Labour Market Issues in Structural Adjustment*. Geneva: International Labour Office.

Ryloh, Robert. 1994. "Restructuring at the National Level: Labour-Led Restructuring and Reform in Australia." In Werner Sengenberger and Duncan Campbell, eds., *Creating Economic Opportunities: The Role of Labour Standards in Industrial Restructuring*. Geneva: International Labour Office.

Thelen, Kathleen. *1991. Union of Parts: Labor Politics in Postwar Germany*. Ithaca, NY: ILR Press/Cornell University.

The Contributors

Roy J. Adams is Professor of Industrial Relations at McMaster University, Hamilton, and a member of the graduate faculty, Centre for Industrial Relations, University of Toronto. He has been a visiting professor at numerous universities around the world, and is the author or co-author of many books and journal articles on labor and employment issues. Dr. Adams also sits on the editorial boards of several distinguished journals, including the *International Journal of Human Resource Management* and the *Canadian Labour and Employment Law Journal*.

Gordon Betcherman is executive Director of the Human Resource Group at Ekos Research Associates and Research Director of the Work Network, Canadian Policy Research Networks. From 1992 to 1994, he was a Senior Fellow in the School of Industrial Relations, Queen's University, Kingston, and from 1987 to 1992, he was a Research Director at the Economic Council of Canada. Dr. Betcherman is a Visiting Fellow at the School of Policy Studies at Queen's University, a Director of the Canadian Employment Research Forum, and co-editor of the journal *Canadian Business Economics*.

Beth Bilson is a Professor of Law at the University of Saskatchewan, and Chairperson of the Saskatchewan Labour Relations Board. She has served as Assistant Vice-President (Administration) of the University of Saskatchewan, as Senior Grievance Officer of the University of Saskatchewan Faculty Association, and as an arbitrator under a number of collective agreements. She has taught in the areas of tort law, labor law, and legal history, and is the author of a number of publications in these areas.

John O'Grady is an independent consultant specializing in labor market and industrial relations issues. In 1992, he was Visiting Senior Researcher at the Economic Council of Canada. From 1987 to 1990, he was Research Director and Legislative Director of the Ontario Federation of Labour. Prior to joining the OFL, he was the representative in Asia for the Canadian Labour Congress and the International Confederation of Free Trade Unions. He has also served as assistant to the President of the Ontario Public Services Employees Union and as an adjunct professor at the Centre for Research on Work and Society at York University.

Roger Phillips is President and Chief Executive Officer, IPSCO Inc. Before joining IPSCO, he was employed by various parts of Alcan Aluminium Ltd. from 1960 to 1981. His last position there was Vice-President and Chief Technical Officer (responsible for technology, research, and engineering); he was also President of its subsidiary, Alcan International Ltd. Mr. Phillips is a member or director of a number of nonprofit organizations and business-related groups, as well as Co-Chairman of the Canadian Steel Trade and Employment Congress, Founding President and Honourary Chairman of the Institute for Saskatchewan Enterprise, and President of the Mel Williamson Foundation.

Members of the
C.D. Howe Institute*

---

* The views expressed in this publication are those of the authors and do not necessarily
  reflect the opinions of the Institute's members.

Clairvest Group Inc.
Cogeco inc.
Consoltex Group Inc.
Consumers Gas
Coopers & Lybrand
E. Kendall Cork
William J. Cosgrove
Co-Steel Inc.
Marcel Côté
Pierre Côté
Cott Beverages Inc.
Crestbrook Forest Industries Ltd.
John Crispo
Devon Gaffney Cross
John Crow
Crown Life Insurance Company Limited
Dai-ichi Life International (Canada), Inc.
Thomas P. d'Aquino
Paul Davidson
Leo de Bever
W. Ross DeGeer
Catherine Delaney
Deloitte & Touche
Desjardins Ducharme Stein Monast
Robert Després
Deutsche Bank (Canada)
Iain St. C. Dobson
The Dominion of Canada General Insurance Company
DuPont Canada Inc.
Marcel Dutil
Gordon H. Eberts
The Empire Life Insurance Company
ENSIS Corporation
Ernst & Young
Export Development Corporation
Ronald J. Farano, Q.C.
First Marathon Securities Limited
Aaron M. Fish
John P. Fisher
Fishery Products International Limited
C.J. Michael Flavell, Q.C.
James Fleck
Ford Motor Company of Canada, Limited
Formula Growth Limited

L. Yves Fortier, C.C., Q.C.
Four Seasons Hotels Limited
GSW Inc.
Jim Garrow
General Electric Canada Inc.
General Motors of Canada Limited
Joseph F. Gill
Gluskin Sheff + Associates Inc.
Goodman & Goodman
Peter Goring
Dr. John A.G. Grant
The Great-West Life Assurance Company
Greyhound Lines of Canada
Morton Gross
Groupe Sobeco Inc.
H. Anthony Hampson
C.M. Harding Foundation
G.R. Heffernan
Lawrence L. Herman
Hewlett-Packard (Canada) Ltd.
Hill & Knowlton Canada
Home Oil Company Limited
Gordon J. Homer
Honeywell Limited
Hongkong Bank of Canada
The Horsham Corporation
Dezsö Horváth
H. Douglas Hunter
Lou Hyndman, Q.C.
IBM Canada Ltd.
Imasco Limited
Imperial Oil Limited
Inco Limited
Inland Cement Limited
The Insurance Bureau of Canada
Interprovincial Pipe Line Inc.
The Investment Funds Institute of Canada
Investors Group Inc.
IPSCO Inc.
Tsutomu Iwasaki
The Jarislowsky Foundation
KPMG Peat Marwick Thorne
Mark D. Kassirer
Joseph Kruger II

R.William Lawson
Jacques A. Lefebvre
Gérard Limoges
Loewen, Ondaatje, McCutcheon Limited
London Life Insurance Company
J.W. (Wes) MacAleer
McCallum Hill Companies
McCarthy Tétrault
W.A. Macdonald
MacDonald, Dettwiler & Associates Ltd.
Bruce M. McKay
McKinsey & Company
Maclab Enterprises
James Maclaren Industries Inc.
Maclean Hunter Limited
Jack M. MacLeod
McMillan Binch
MacMillan Bloedel Limited
William Mackness
Mannville Oil & Gas Ltd.
The Manufacturers Life Insurance
 Company
Maple Leaf Foods Inc.
Dr. Georg Marais
Maritime Telegraph & Telephone
 Company, Limited
Marsh & McLennan Limited
Master Equity Investments Inc.
James Mauldin
The Mercantile and General
 Reinsurance Group
William M. Mercer Limited
Merck Frosst Canada Inc.
Methanex Corporation
Micmac Maliseet Development
 Corporation Inc.
Miles Canada Inc.
Robert Mitchell Inc.
The Molson Companies Limited
Monsanto Canada Inc.
Montreal Trust
Moore Corporation Limited
The Mutual Life Assurance Company of
 Canada
National Trust
National Westminster Bank of Canada
Nesbitt Thomson Deacon

E.P. Neufeld
Newcourt Credit Group Inc.
Noma Industries Limited
Noranda Forest Inc.
Noranda Inc.
North American Life Assurance
 Company
Northwood Pulp and Timber Limited
NOVA Corporation of Alberta
Ontario Hydro
The Oshawa Group Limited
Katsuhiko Otaki
James S. Palmer
PanCanadian Petroleum Limited
Pembina Corporation
Petro-Canada
Philips, Hager & North Investment
 Management Ltd.
Pirie Foundation
Les Placements T.A.L. Ltée.
Placer Dome Inc.
Power Corporation of Canada
PowerWest Financial Ltd.
Pratt & Whitney Canada Inc.
Price Waterhouse
J. Robert S. Prichard
Procor Limited
ProGas Limited
QUNO Corporation
RBC Dominion Securities Inc.
Redpath Industries Limited
Henri Remmer
Retail Council of Canada
Richardson Greenshields
 of Canada Limited
R.T. Riley
Robin Hood Multifoods Inc.
Rogers Communications Inc.
Rothschild Canada Limited
Royal Bank of Canada
ROYCO Hotels & Resorts
St. Lawrence Cement Inc.
Samuel, Son & Co., Limited
Sandwell Inc.
Sanpalo Investments Corporation
Guylaine Saucier
André Saumier

Sceptre Investment Counsel
Sceptre Resources Limited
Dick Schmeelk
ScotiaMcLeod Inc.
Sharwood and Company
Shell Canada Limited
Sherritt Inc.
Sidbec-Dosco Inc.
Sierra Systems Consultants Inc.
SNC Lavalin Inc.
Southam Inc.
Spar Aerospace Limited
Speirs Consultants Inc.
Philip Spencer, Q.C.
The Standard Life Assurance Company
Strategico Inc.
Sun Life Assurance Company of Canada
Suncor Inc.
Swiss Bank Corporation (Canada)
TELUS Corporation
Laurent Thibault
Thornmark Corporation
3M Canada Inc.
The Toronto Dominion Bank

The Toronto Stock Exchange
Torstar Corporation
TransAlta Utilities Corporation
TransCanada PipeLines Limited
Trimac Limited
Trizec Corporation Ltd.
Robert J. Turner
Unilever Canada Limited
Urgel Bourgie Limitée
Vancouver Stock Exchange
Gustavo Vega Cánovas
VIA Rail Canada Inc.
J.H. Warren
West Fraser Timber Co. Ltd.
Westcoast Energy Inc.
Weston Forest Corporation
George Weston Limited
Alfred G. Wirth
M.K. Wong & Associates Ltd.
Wood Gundy Inc.
Fred R. Wright
Xerox Canada Inc.
Paul H. Ziff

Honorary Members

G. Arnold Hart
David Kirk

Paul H. Leman
J. Ross Tolmie, Q.C.

Publications in
"The Social Policy Challenge"

Already Published

1   Watson, William G., John Richards, and David M. Brown. *The Case for Change: Reinventing the Welfare State* (1994). 134 pp.; $12.95. ISBN 0-88806-336-9.

2   Green, Christopher, et al. *Unemployment Insurance: How to Make It Work* (1994). 200 pp. $14.95. ISBN 0-88806-338-5.

3   Harris, Richard G., et al. *Paying Our Way: The Welfare State in Hard Times* (1994). 138 pp.; $12.95. ISBN 0-88806-340-7.

4   Courchene, Thomas J. *Social Canada in the Millennium: Reform Imperatives and Restructuring Principles* (1994). 368 pp.; $19.95. ISBN 0-88806-355-5.

5   Richards, John, et al. *Helping the Poor: A Qualified Case for "Workfare"* (1995). 206 pp.; $14.95. ISBN 0-88806341-5.

6   Fallis, George, et al. *Home Remedies: Rethinking Canadian Housing Policy* (1995). 244 pp.; $14.95. ISBN 0-88806-353-9.

7   Thomason, Terry, et al. *Chronic Stress: Workers' Compensation in the 1990s* (1995). 178 pp.; $14.95. ISBN 0-88806-357-1.

8   Dooley, Martin D., et al. *Family Matters: New Policies for Divorce, Lone Mothers, and Child Poverty* (1995). 290 pp.; $16.95. ISBN 0-88806-354-7.

9   May, Doug, and Alton Hollett, with Brian Lee Crowley and Lars Osberg. *The Rock in a Hard Place: Atlantic Canada and the UI Trap* (1995). 245 pp.; $14.95. ISBN 0-88806-356-3.

10 Adams, Roy J., Gordon Betcherman, and Beth Bilson, with Roger Phillips and John O'Grady. *Good Jobs, Bad Jobs, No Jobs: Tough Choices for Canadian Labor Law* (1995). 198 pp.; $14.95. ISBN 0-88806-352-0.